Contemporary Wales
Volume 15

CONTRIBUTIONS TO CONTEMPORARY WALES

The editor, Richard Wyn Jones, is always pleased to receive papers on any topic relating to the economy, society and politics of Wales for consideration for publication in *Contemporary Wales*.

Submission of papers:
All articles are subject to a refereeing process. Contributions should be written in a style which makes them readily accessible to non-specialists. The editor is very willing, if desired, to discuss proposals for papers with intending authors. Further details regarding submission and preparation of articles are to be found on the *Contemporary Wales* website:
www.contemporary-wales.com
or contact the editor at the Institute of Welsh Politics, Department of International Politics, University of Wales, Aberystwyth, SY23 3DB.

Subscriptions:
Subscription for one volume per annum is £6.50, and the price is otherwise £7.50. Payment is required with all orders and may be made by sterling cheque (payable to the University of Wales Press), Giro (account 494 9056), credit card (Visa or Mastercard). Apply to Journal Subscriptions at the University of Wales Press, 10 Columbus Walk, Brigantine Place, Cardiff, CF10 4UP, tel: 029 2049 6899, fax: 029 2049 6109, e-mail *journals@press.wales.ac.uk*

Advertisements:
Advertisements are welcome and rates will be quoted on request. Enquiries should be made to the Deputy Director at the University of Wales Press at the address given above.

Acknowledgements:
The editor would like to thank all those who have acted as referees for this volume. I am also grateful for the invaluable assistance provided in the editing of this volume by Emeritus Professor John Black, Honorary Departmental Fellow in the Department of Economics, University of Wales, Aberystwyth, and Gwenan Creunant, Administrator of the Institute of Welsh Politics, University of Wales, Aberystwyth.

CONTEMPORARY WALES

An annual review of economic,
political and social research

Volume 15

Editor

Richard Wyn Jones

*Published on behalf of the Board of Celtic Studies
of the University of Wales*

**Cardiff
University of Wales Press
2002**

www.wales.ac.uk/press

Published January 2003

British Library Cataloguing in Publication Data
A catalogue record for this book is available from the British Library.

ISBN 0-7083-1809-6

ISSN 0951-4937

Cover design and photograph by Marian Delyth
Typeset by Bryan Turnbull
Printed in Wales by Dinefwr Press, Llandybïe

CONTENTS

CONTRIBUTORS

John Bachtler is Professor and Head of Department at the European Policies Research Centre, University of Strathclyde in Glasgow. He specializes in comparative research on regional policies in Europe, and EU regional policy in particular.

Graham Benfield is the Chief Executive of Wales Council for Voluntary Action, and has over twenty-five years of management, policy, project and community development experience in London, Plymouth, Liverpool and Wales.

David Brooksbank is Professor of Enterprise and Small Business Economics at the University of Glamorgan Business School and Director of the Welsh Enterprise Institute. He has published widely on enterprise and entrepreneurship, economic regeneration, unemployment policies and trends in the Welsh economy.

Chris Burns is Head of Policy at Caerphilly County Borough Council. A graduate in Economics and History from the University of Wales, Cardiff, he has spent most of his career working in the field of economic development, tourism and community regeneration.

John Clarke is Chief Executive of the Welsh European Funding Office (WEFO) and took up his duties in March 2000. Formerly a career banker, John was for eight years Barclays' Regional Director in the East Midlands and later in Wales.

Alistair Cole has been a lecturer in Politics and French Politics at Merton College, Oxford, and the Universities of Aston, Keele and Bradford before he joined the School of European Studies at Cardiff University in 1999 as Professorial Fellow. He publishes widely in the sphere of French and European Politics.

David Denver is a Professor at the Department of Politics and International Relations, Lancaster University. He is series editor of the *British Elections and Parties Review* and convenes the elections group of the Political Studies Association. He specializes in elections and voting behaviour and also has a research interest in Scottish politics.

Michael German is the Leader of the Liberal Democrats in the National Assembly and directed the Welsh Liberal Democrats' general election campaigns in 1992 and 1997. He is a former chair of the Objective 3 Monitoring Committee, and his interests include skills development in small and large companies in Wales.

J. Barry Jones has been Director of the Welsh Governance Centre at Cardiff University since its establishment in 1999. He has published widely on European regionalism, the Labour Party and devolution, and is joint editor of two recent studies of Welsh politics: *The Road to the National Assembly for Wales* (2000, with Denis Balsom) and *Inclusive Government and Party Management* (2001, with John Osmond).

John Loughlin is a Professor of European Politics at Cardiff University, and currently holds the European Commission's Jean Monnet Chair of European Political Economy. His main research interests are in regionalism, nationalism and federalism and the changing nature of the nation-state in western Europe.

Iain MacAllister is a Research Associate in the Department of International Politics and International Relations, Lancaster University. He has co-authored articles in the *British Journal of Political Science and Electoral Studies* and is currently writing a book on the Liberal Democrats to be published in early 2003.

Peter Midmore is Professor of Applied Economics at the University of Wales, Aberystwyth. His main interests are in rural and regional economics, and he is currently coordinator of a European Commission contract to investigate the relations between organic farming initiatives and rural development in nineteen countries.

Kevin Morgan is Professor of European Regional Development in the Department of City and Regional Planning at Cardiff University. He was a member of the Task and Finish Group which the National Assembly set up to examine the teething problems with the Objective 1 programme in 2001.

Richard Rawlings is Professor of Law at the London School of Economics. His main interests are in the field of public law, and more recently, he has been researching in the sphere of devolution with particular reference to Wales. Present research interests include topics in administrative law and the relation between European Union law and the national constitution.

Alan Storer is a postgraduate research student at the School of European Studies, Cardiff University, and his research interests are in the fields of Welsh politics, British territorial governance and the relationship between politics and business.

Colin Williams is Professor in the Department of Welsh at Cardiff University and is a world-renowned authority on linguistic minorities and language planning. He is the author of numerous articles on the sociology of language, and his main focus of research is the place of Welsh in contemporary Wales and comparing the linguistic situation in Wales with other parts of the world.

Phil Williams is a space scientist and a Professor in the Physics Department of the University of Wales, Aberystwyth. He is a Plaid Cymru Assembly Member for South Wales East, and since 1992, has been spokesperson on energy and the environment.

Editor's Note

Richard Rawlings's article 'The New Model Wales' (*Journal of Law and Society*, 25, 4, 1998), remains the best treatment so far of the Byzantine complexities of our post-devolution constitutional order. That this analysis was published before the election of the first members of the National Assembly and has yet proven so prescient in its tracing of the contours of post-devolution politics is vivid testimony to Rawlings's acuity. All students of contemporary Wales have cause for rejoicing that 2003 will witness the appearance of his monograph *Delineating Wales* as the fourth publication in the Politics and Society in Wales book series recently established by the Social Science Committee of the University of Wales Board of Celtic Studies. In the interim, it is a cause of considerable pleasure that this journal is able to publish a version of Richard Rawlings's O'Donnell lecture delivered in a number of the constituent institutions of the University of Wales earlier in 2002. Given that the commission chaired by Lord Richard is currently deliberating the powers of the National Assembly, Rawlings's typically nuanced yet incisive treatment of the evolution of the devolved body should prove especially timely.

Equally timely is the special section included in this issue of *Contemporary Wales* offering different perspectives on the experience so far of the Objective One European Structural Fund programme for west Wales and the Valleys. While the views put forward in the various contributions are certainly varied, the overall impression gleaned from them is concerning. Much remains to be done if the (arguably over-inflated) expectations surrounding this programme are to be realized.

The special section is based on contributions to a special conference organized by the Institute of Welsh Politics in the University of Wales, Aberystwyth, in conjunction with Cardiff University's Regeneration Institute, at the Cwmaman Institute. I would like to take this opportunity to thank all those involved in the organization of the conference, in particular the Director of the Regeneration Institute, Professor Kevin Morgan,

Gwenan Creunant from the Institute of Welsh Politics, who shouldered almost all the organizational burden, and all those in Cwmaman who provided such a memorably warm welcome to the conference-goers.

Richard Wyn Jones
Editor

1. TOWARDS A PARLIAMENT – THREE FACES OF THE NATIONAL ASSEMBLY FOR WALES

(*The 2001 O'Donnell Lecture*)

Richard Rawlings

It is a great honour to be here, in the land of my birth and upbringing, as one in a long line of O'Donnell lecturers in the University of Wales. The list is a remarkable one, both for the many distinguished lecturers and for the range of subject matter, from 'The Pastoral tradition and its influence on the Welsh way of life' to 'The Welsh in London'; and 'The medieval Welsh idea of law' to 'Space invaders – the Welsh in English politics'.

It is, however, worth reflecting on the terms of the O'Donnell bequest, which lays down the field within which each lecturer is expected to find a subject: 'The British or Celtic element in the English language and the dialects of English counties; the special terms and words used in agriculture and handicrafts; the British or Celtic element in the existing population of England.' At this point I have to confess to a serious breach of trust. Analysing the Welsh devolutionary development by reference to 'the special terms and words used in agriculture' etc. has proved beyond my limited powers. The pervasive sense of the bequest, faithfully reflected in many of the previous lecture titles, is of a Wales – whenever it was – hanging on; and further of vestiges, perhaps 'Welsh surnames in the Shropshire parish registers' or 'Celtic traces in the English Lake counties'. In contrast, I am encouraged by members of the University of Wales Board of Celtic Studies to engage with a contemporary Wales seeking to make its way in the world. That is, in the context of a devolution, which – however critical one cares to be of the constitutional design and practical workings – amounts in terms of the historical development of Wales to a political metamorphosis.

The dictionary definition of devolution as 'the process of transferring power from central government to a lower or regional level' (Robertson,

1993) is less than illuminating. It is not only too limited, effectively draining the devolutionary process of social, cultural and economic meaning, but also too general, glossing over the fact, central to this lecture, that devolutionary schemes come in all shapes and sizes. Ten, twenty, certainly fifty years from now, the trajectory of the O'Donnell lecture series will be an interesting litmus test of the scale of Welsh reinvention and renewal following on the establishment of Wales's own first democratically elected and accountable government.

The subject of this lecture is the design and internal development of the National Assembly for Wales, and in particular the key issue of its constitutional trajectory. The discussion is divided into two main parts. In Part 1 three competing constitutional models of the Assembly are specified – ideal types. A conceptual framework is thus put in place for evaluating the continuing evolution of the internal architecture, most obviously in terms of the title of the lecture, 'Towards a Parliament'. In Part 2 the play and interplay of the three models, and in particular how this reflects and reinforces an underlying trajectory, is examined by reference to a series of developments, political, legal and institutional, some well known, others less so. Put together, these elements amount to nothing less than a form of constitution building for Wales, in part by stealth, or in silence.

It is idle to think in terms of a single controlling mind: would that there was one! In the corridors of Cardiff Bay there is much whispering about 'the project' – legal, administrative and constitutional expansionism on the part of the Assembly – but with no clearly articulated destination in view. One has instead to think in terms of layers of explanation, meaning, for example, the personal as well as the political, individual predilections being especially important in the small infant body; or the administrative together with the legal, the perceived lack of policy-making capacity in the Assembly administration being a dominant concern in this formative period.

Wales currently has a form of government that may safely be described as like nothing else on earth: *De jure* a corporate body, though increasingly a corporate shell; a jigsaw of powers, of a thousand pieces and more; an umbilical cord joining ministers and members constituted by a system of subject committees; these are bare outlines of what elsewhere I describe as 'a strange anatomy' (Rawlings, forthcoming; Williams, 1999). Naturally this has been shaped by many diverse factors: a mix of the positive and responsive, some general in character, some particular to Wales. An Assembly, not a Parliament as in Scotland, has been justified on grounds of limited consensus for change and – redolent of the terms of the O'Donnell bequest

– closer integration with England. The devolutionary scheme thus presents a dual character: transformative, when read in light of the retarded development of a distinctive Welsh polity, limited or 'gentler' devolution in the context of a reinvented Union State.

A vital feature is the existence of major gaps or silences in the devolution legislation, the fact that so much has been open to contention. 'A process not an event' (Davies, 1999): the architecture of the scheme reflects and re-inforces an evolutionary approach with an inbuilt capacity for change. Expressed slightly differently, the Government of Wales Act 1998 (GWA) should be seen – like so many constitutional documents – as both limiting and liberating, a cautious measure that nonetheless has provided a frame-work within which the Assembly can develop organically (see Patchett, 2000).

For laboratory testing of a new set of constitutional arrangements, all those experiments with constants and variables, the contemporary Welsh experience could scarcely be bettered. In three short years Wales has seen minority administration under the pre-existing UK government rep-resentative; a constitutional coup and minority administration with a more popular leader; and coalition government with that same leader and the working majority that had been assumed in the original design. This politically circuitous route is one that has left deep marks in terms of the Assembly's internal development.

Lawyers are fond of disclaimers. The discussion that follows is not one in favour of the current model of executive devolution. The approach is one of constructive engagement with the devolutionary scheme under which the people of Wales are presently governed. I also make no apology for concentrating on the constitutional and institutional aspects. As well as the fact that these represent my own discipline, many years of research and teaching in public law and administration have convinced me of the futility of treating the process and product of policy-making as if they were in two separate compartments.

Much has been said and written, by me and others (Rawlings, 2001; see NAW, 2002a) about the vexed question of increased legislative powers – primary or otherwise, according to a pragmatic or principled design – for the Assembly. Notably, however, the essential parameters of that debate, the dichotomy of legislative and executive devolution, tend to obscure the scope for variation in substance and style under both models, and even for a devolutionary development of mix and match. Perhaps, hopefully, the up-coming independent commission on the powers and electoral arrangements of the Assembly will have more on its plate than is commonly imagined (Welsh Labour Party and Welsh Liberal Democrats, 2000).

This lecture is consciously designed to promote a more general discussion, one that extends beyond the formal question of powers to the internal constitutional and administrative arrangements of the new Welsh polity. It is important not to lose sight of the wider picture here. While it is possible to argue for a more parliamentary form of architecture but without parliamentary powers in the guise of legislative devolution, it would be foolish to overlook the synergy of style and substance, by which is meant the general sense – or calculation – that expanding parliamentary style elements in the Assembly helps to ease the path to having an actual Parliament for Wales.

1. THREE FACES OF THE ASSEMBLY

The concept of the 'body corporate' (see GWA, Ch. 38, 1998, s1.(2) and Roddick, 1999) may be likened to a formal legal mask, behind which the Assembly in ideal-typical fashion has presented three faces. The interplay between these different constitutional models, their waxing and waning, as well as the interface with the *de jure* concept, with which they fit more or less comfortably, effectively charts the internal development of the new representative body.

First face: Welsh Office plus

The first face represents a minimalist view of the new constitutional design. The structures and processes are seen as a makeover, so demonstrating much in the way of political and administrative continuity. This is epitomized in the original design feature of substitution, or the grounding of the scheme in the powers and responsibilities of the Secretary of State for Wales (NAW, 1999 and see Lambert, 2001). From this perspective, it is a case of the 'Welsh Office plus', the Assembly being treated as an add-on to, or reinvention of, the pre-existing model of territorial administration – a specific cure for the particular malady of a democratic deficit.

A chief characteristic of the model is the powerful role of the Assembly First Secretary (seen here as the lineal descendant of the UK government representative). In turn, the Assembly may be said to have an essentially advisory function, not only in the case of the subject committees, but also in plenary session. Related features are a limited role for cabinet (emphatically not a case of *primus inter pares*) and a strict view of the functions of the Presiding Officer (no great sympathy for separation of powers).

The model can be seen as indicative of the Assembly under the first First Secretary, Alun Michael. That is, to anticipate the argument, cautious and centralist, a very personal or 'hands-on' style of management. But, further, it can be seen to fit perfectly well with the formal constitutional design of the devolution statute, for example, in terms of the routing of the system of delegations via the Assembly First Secretary (GWA, Ch. 38, 1998, s.62), as also in an electoral system originally calculated to produce majority government (Welsh Labour Party, 1997; Jones and Balsom, 2000; Morgan and Mungham, 2000).

One should not underestimate the forces of inertia. As every student of government knows, it is one thing to move chairs round, quite another to alter professional habits and mindsets. Rightly, successive Permanent Secretaries have emphasized the challenges to a bureaucratic culture entailed in Welsh devolution. How could it be otherwise given the historical legacy of the administrative character of the Welsh Office, or what erstwhile Permanent Secretary Rachel Lomax memorably referred to as its 'colonial' role: transmitting London policy to Wales (Laffin, 2002)? That for obvious reasons the model of 'Welsh Office plus' has not been publicly articulated is no measure of its official potency.

Second face: corporate/collaborative
The second face represents the idea of a newly textured democratic culture: consensual and collaborative, inclusive and cross-party in terms of the structures and processes. As such, it featured strongly in the public discussion ahead of devolution, being indicative of the work of the National Assembly Advisory Group (NAAG, 1998; MacAllister, 2000: Chaney and Fevre, 2001) as promoted by the then secretary of state for Wales, Ron Davies. It is appropriately labelled the designer-friendly face of the Assembly.

This model is about taking the concept of the corporate body seriously. Whereas under the first model the concept is essentially there to fill the (legal) space vacated by the Welsh Secretary, great stress is laid here on the role and authority of the Assembly qua Assembly, and on the (policy development) work of the all-party subject committees. In conjunction, that is, with the late tilt in the devolutionary scheme in favour of a cabinet system (GWA, Ch. 38, 1998, ss.53, 56–7, and see Rawlings, 1998). Determinedly non-Westminster in style and orientation, this is the Welsh constitutional hybrid splendidly envisioned.

The argumentation betrays, in the case of NAAG, a certain naivety and lack of constitutional understanding. The capacity of the Westminster-style parliamentary tradition to reinvent itself in other settings was grossly underestimated. All the more so, it may be said, when many of the most senior Assembly members have had substantial Westminster experience, and in a situation where the main opposition party – Plaid Cymru – is seeking a Parliament for Wales (Jones, 2001). Again, NAAG glossed over the question of how far the Assembly would be able to operate on different constitutional assumptions to Westminster and Whitehall when, by reason of the scheme of executive devolution, it was so heavily dependent on the centre for political and administrative collaboration and support.

For the avoidance of doubt, it was never a question of importing Westminster lock, stock and barrel. An element of proportional representation and greater gender balance, a less stuffy atmosphere: in various ways the opportunity has been taken to style the Assembly for a new millennium, and rightly so. Nonetheless, it is fair to say that the extravagant version of the body corporate – 'a new kind of politics in Wales' – was always stretching credulity.

Third face: parliamentary or 'government and opposition'
The third face is more familiar, that is, from the viewpoint of comparative constitutional design and development. It represents the basic outlines of a parliamentary system, premised first on the operational independence of the presiding chair and clerks, and second on the practice and conventions of cabinet government. It is also indicative in the Assembly of an enhanced scrutiny role for the subject committees, and in an improved range of parliamentary services for individual members. A sense of government and opposition pervades many of the structures and processes.

Emblematic of what I have called the 'strange anatomy', this is also the model that does not sit easily with the formal constitutional design of the devolution statute. So, to promote it, there is a need carefully to distinguish the de facto from the *de jure*. And this, to anticipate the discussion, is a defining feature of the constitutional trajectory of the Assembly in its formative period (Jones and Osmond, 2001).

Once again, this face need not be cast in the particular Westminster mould – as familiarly associated with a largely adversarial two-party system and by a peculiarly strong form of executive domination by the party in power. Parliaments come in all shapes and sizes, including perhaps in Wales.

Constitutional trilemma
Reconciliation of some demands of the competing models is clearly possible. As First Minister, Rhodri Morgan has promoted the idea of the

Assembly cabinet 'as a government delivering'. But he has also rightly stressed the need in a small country like Wales to harness all talents in the political process (Morgan, 2000). That the general contours of a parliamentary system should not harden into a rigid, formalistic and overly exclusive system is a vital concern.

Other tensions between the models are more intractable, such that accentuating the features or moulding the structures and procedures in the image of one face serves to disfigure another. One example is the evident tension between a strong centralized form of decision-making and the more open and participatory process that people were led to expect in the White Paper, *A Voice for Wales*. So also the parliamentary-style model is indicative of a restricted role for backbenchers. There has been, to coin a phrase, a 'constitutional trilemma' at the heart of the devolutionary development in Wales.

The three models further highlight the dynamic or uninterrupted nature of the process of internal constitutional design. The so-called 'devolution settlement' has actually entailed a fluid mix of competing architectural and procedural forms. As indicated, the initial sense of an administrative and political makeover has been successfully – and in my view rightly – challenged. Pressures for change reflect a greater concern for responsible and effective modalities of government, consistent with the ideals of parliamentary democracy.

2. PLAY AND INTERPLAY

So far from representing a steady state, the current position shows a diverse pattern of incremental change (G. P. Davies, 2000; Sherlock, 2000). The recent internal Assembly review of procedure (NAW, 2002a; Jones and Osmond, 2002) is but one element in this, and the looming independent commission will be confronted by it, however narrowly the self-styled 'Welsh Assembly Government'[1] wishes to limit the inquiry. Where else to begin, then, than with the fall of Alun Michael, in more ways than one a very constitutional coup?

The fall of Alun Michael

According to the Presiding Officer, Lord Elis-Thomas, it was 'the first day of devolution' (Elis-Thomas, 2000). A tendentious view, but one that reflects the competing constitutional models specified in this lecture; it will echo across the pages of Welsh history.

One way of characterizing Alun Michael's approach is in terms of devolution as the done deed. That is, an effort to dampen down the ongoing process of devolutionary change, or more positively, a premium on political and administrative continuity justified on the basis of a need for stability for the infant body (Michael, 1999). Typically, it also involved proceeding inside the Assembly in accordance with a strong hierarchical view of the corporate body ('Welsh Office plus'). Far from exploring the boundaries, it was a case of an already attenuated devolutionary scheme writ small.

The great constitutional and political paradox of this first period is shown. Cautious and controlling, by bearing down so hard or effectively slowing the development of a new Welsh polity above and beyond machinery to implement or manage centrally devised policies, the administration of Alun Michael served to heighten the underlying tensions in Cardiff Bay. Via a slow-burning fuse, matters would explode in what is aptly called – in the devolutionary sense – the first Welsh constitutional crisis (Laffin, 2001). Who would have believed it?

The detail of the fall will no doubt continue to fascinate. Yet there is clearly a wider significance: first, as regards the character or quality of the Welsh devolutionary development, both in general and at a formative period; and, second, in terms of the knock-on effects, institutional and otherwise, and especially for an autochthonous process of constitution-building.

In the short term, the advent of Rhodri Morgan as First Minister heralded a reworked form of (Labour) minority administration in the Assembly: a shift from one-off agreements towards an informal cohabitation arrangement involving Plaid Cymru (Osmond, 2000). One is tempted to describe this as replacing a 'red light' theory of devolution, minimalist and exhibiting a strong measure of internal hierarchical control, with an 'amber light' view, licence to proceed. Again, the arrival on the scene some six months later of the coalition or partnership government of Labour and the Liberal Democrats could be said to have ushered in 'green light' conditions for Assembly policy-making and administration, a more dynamic approach. This is not to overlook the huge constraints entailed in the Welsh devolutionary scheme. Quite the reverse – it is only in this third period that the limitations as well as the many opportunities involved in the devolved system of government could be fully tested.

That Alun Michael's demise was triggered by a classic issue of inter-governmental relations – fiscal transfer or guarantee[2] – gives the affair an extra poignancy. Effectively, his special case for exercising power of a close insider or 'sweetheart' relationship with (Labour) colleagues in London was overborne by expanding forces for increased territorial autonomy. Looked at 'top-down' (from the UK perspective), the constitutional coup that overthrew him represents the loss of a measure of control by the centre; while, seen 'bottom-up' (in terms of the local constitutional development), it shows the Assembly flexing its muscles as a distinctive polity – less deferential (Marinetto, 2001; Cole and Storer, 2002).

Reference here to the three competing models demonstrates how the internal development of the Assembly has been more complicated than first appears. Alun Michael not only practised proprietorial government but also preached the virtues of consensus and inclusiveness (Michael, 1999). Effectively tarred with the same brush, the designer-friendly model has not had much of an opportunity to shine, the counter-reaction being very much in favour of a parliamentary style model. Such, anyway, has been the lament of Ron Davies (R, Davies, 2000).

Put another way, the early quest for a newly textured democratic culture glossed over the pull not only of the (Westminster) parliamentary tradition, but also, in the Presiding Officer's words, of 'the territorial administrative/ executive government in the previous system' (Elis-Thomas, 2001a) or, as I prefer, the model of 'Welsh Office plus'. By in a very real sense reliving the past, the first Assembly administration did little for the idea of a distinctive constitutional future premised on new-style modalities or forms of government. The greatest legacy of Alun Michael is the firm impetus given to the cause of a Parliament for Wales. It is a fine irony.

The rise of the presiding office

Effectively giving the Assembly a more parliamentary face, the rise of what was formerly called 'OPO', the Office of the Presiding Officer, involves a series of elements. There is a firmer insistence on the separateness or – as Lord Elis-Thomas would prefer – independence of the office from the Assembly administration. An enhanced role and status for the clerk to the Assembly is constitutionally speaking very significant, as is the arrival on the scene of an independent legal adviser.[3] Organizational change inside what is now called the Presiding Office is a key indicator, not least a more than doubling of the original staff complement (Rawlings, forthcoming). The office has gained substantial additional responsibilities, marking a more expansive approach to the provision of parliamentary-style services.

Events leading up to the fall of Alun Michael, procedural wrangles and exceptional political pressures sorely tested the role and standing of this pole of Assembly authority. Conversely, the coup gave the Presiding Officer the perfect opportunity to play the parliamentary card. The vision presented was one of separate budgets, clear procedural and operational autonomy and discrete control of the 'parliamentary' buildings in Cardiff Bay (NAW, 2000a; Elis-Thomas, 2001b) which, translated, means a push for the fledgling institution more into the mainstream of comparative constitutional development, not least in the countries of the Commonwealth.

A subsequent feature all too rare in the Welsh devolutionary development – clear articulation of a set of constitutional principles (NAW, 2000b) – serves to illustrate how much of this has come to pass: 'The Presiding Officer holds the position equivalent to the Speaker in Parliament, carrying out his role independently of the Assembly's Executive.' 'His function, and that of his Office (OPO) is to represent the interests of all Assembly Members and to ensure that the business of the Assembly is discharged smoothly and impartially and in keeping with the best traditions of representative institutions.' 'OPO has the role of ensuring that Assembly Members can effectively scrutinize the work of the Assembly's Executive.' The unexceptional character of these propositions – that is to those reared on basic canons of parliamentary government – makes the point.

Great ingenuity has been shown in the so-called 'separation project' (Rawlings, forthcoming). A raft of service-level agreements between the Presiding Office and core divisions of the Welsh Assembly Government put the flesh on the bones. Today, incorporating the chamber and committee secretariats and the table office, and now boasting a corporate services division as well as the Assembly communication services, the Presiding Office increasingly looks like a professional corps and core of authority for a National Assembly worthy of the name. Not, however, that there is a clean break from the administrative arm of the Welsh Assembly Government, something which is legally impossible to achieve in view of corporate status and in particular of overreaching membership of the Home Civil Service.

More recent developments confirm the rise of the Presiding Office. It has, for example, become ever more heavily engaged in the ongoing struggle of the Assembly to win the hearts and minds of the Welsh people. An original objective, 'to make the Assembly accessible by providing information to the public', is today a more proactive one, 'to raise public awareness and understanding of the Assembly and its work'.[4] However attenuated in legal powers, the Assembly should not knowingly be undersold!

The Assembly review of procedure, in seeking to underpin the role of the subject committees especially in matters of scrutiny and legislative development, clearly signals additional resources: more specialist and legal support services for members (NAW, 2002a). It may be modest provision, but once again the parliamentary 'feel' of the institution – alternative sources in 'the legislative branch' of advice and assistance – is enhanced. Different but related to this, there is now all-party agreement by way of formal resolution in favour of 'the clearest possible separation between the Government and the Assembly which is achievable under current legislation' (NAW, 2002b).

It is a long way here from the model of 'Welsh Office plus'. Yet the development is not played out; that is assuming a proper review of the devolution legislation. Fortunately a solution lies close to the hand in the form of a corporate body: not, one hastens to add, the 'all-singing and all-dancing' Assembly corporate form, but in the guise, say, of the Scottish parliamentary corporation, by which is meant the more familiar constitutional model of a distinct legal entity charged with ensuring the service and support of the parliamentary process and associated activities.[5] It is in fact the model originally advocated for the Assembly by a Labour backbench MP, one Rhodri Morgan.[6]

The pursuit of cabinet government
Although the trend to strengthen the political centre inside the corporate body predates the infant's birth, it was predictable that the coalition between Labour and the Liberal Democrats would enhance it, so hastening the move towards a de facto form of parliamentary-type government. Including, that is, by promoting executive rule or dominance through the cabinet system, as well as political stability, with all which that implies for policy development and implementation, and for the conduct of Assembly business.

These vital developments, however, should not be allowed to obscure the flanking institutional and administrative ones. There is major synergy, which has further contributed – in what I call 'the pursuit of cabinet government' – to a significant expansion and empowerment of the executive core of the Assembly. Typically, the process is ongoing.

The dynamic has a special resonance, by reason, on the one hand, of the diffuse or strong committee model originally envisaged for the Assembly, and, on the other hand, of the perceived lack of policy-making capacity in the old territorial department (Morgan, 2000). And, once again, such raising of the inner capacities of the devolved administration has evident potentialities for the future constitutional development of Wales.

Turning first to the cabinet, the need to clarify structural arrangements and, further, to formalize political understandings was clearly articulated in the partnership agreement of the two governing parties, *Putting Wales First* (Welsh Labour Party and Welsh Liberal Democrats, 2000). In the event, the subsequent *Protocol for Partnership Government in the Assembly*[7] does not so much draw on the coalition agreement between Labour and the Liberal Democrats in Scotland as import large chunks of it. Seen in historical perspective, this is a classic example of Welsh actors following in the foot-steps of their (constitutionally more advanced) northern cousins. Yet the Scottish arrangements are obviously a product of, and designed for, a different form of devolution settlement, as epitomized in the formal legal separation of the Parliament and the Executive (Scottish Labour Party and Scottish Liberal Democrats, 1999; Goldenberg, 1999). Turning the argument round, the invocation of such arrangements in the case of Wales once again reflects and reinforces a move towards parliamentary-type government, as measured in the increasingly tangible distance between the Assembly's de facto executive and legislature; that is, by effectively concretizing the constitutional system of cabinet government.

So are born Welsh constitutional conventions. 'Cabinet members must at all times and in consistent terms support the decisions which other Cabinet Members have made, whether individually (under delegated authority) or collectively';[8] it could have come from the textbook (and probably did). Nor is the way in which, according to the classical definition, 'the cabinet acts as a political link between the executive and the parliament because ministers are answerable to the parliament' (Bogdanor, 1991) neglected. The *Protocol* identifies various mechanisms of individual accountability, some mandated by the devolution statute, others not.

Speaking more generally, the fact of the partnership government has served to underwrite the appeal of the classical cabinet model of *primus inter pares*, in contrast, one is tempted to add, to contemporary UK experience. From divided patronage to no monopoly of information, and on through an internal norm of comity or mutual co-operation between the partners, the provisions of the *Protocol* brilliantly illustrate how contrasting leadership styles in the Assembly are the product of political and constitutional circumstance as well as personal factors. Put simply, whereas the first First Minister found himself surrounded by colleagues who were lacking in governmental experience, his successor has had to navigate the sensitivities familiarly associated with coalition government.[9] RIP Alun Michael.

Happening at the same time as the coalition government, the establishment of a cabinet executive was taken forward – in accordance with his organizational and management responsibilities – by Permanent Secretary Jon Shortridge. It is a happy juxtaposition, with a political centre more determined and better placed to (be seen to) make a difference now being matched by a more integrated and cohesive system of official advice and support for cabinet (Storer and Lang, 2001).

The major component that is the cabinet secretariat has kept on growing, not simply in terms of staff numbers but also through a widening and deepening of functions: from ministerial support to correspondence management, and on through the routine of Assembly business to handling complex issues of intergovernmental relations. So also, and typical of the age, the communications directorate has been given a high priority. From First Minister's media briefings to formal cabinet statements, and on through to strategy for engaging with an Anglo-centric media,[10] such today is the very public paraphernalia of the Welsh system of cabinet government. Then there is the policy unit, at first a modest affair, but now significantly revamped to incorporate the cabinet's special advisers, another successful breed, and made accountable directly to the First Minister.

A basic governmental apparatus is emerging: in miniature or microcosm. The examples can be multiplied: perhaps the arrival on the scene of deputy ministers (nowhere mentioned in the devolution legislation), or else an emergent system of cabinet subcommittees largely focused on policy development and longer-term strategic thinking.[11] At which point it is important to stress that the Assembly was starting from an exceptionally low base, such was the minimalist staffing and resources of the Welsh Office. Much of the institutional and administrative growth is what should be happening, that is, if one takes the ongoing cause of Welsh devolution seriously.

The process is a somewhat painful one, including in terms of political and administrative friction at the heart of the machine. But enough has been said to show how the quest for ways of 'making a difference', a chief priority of the partnership government, is working to promote a substantial thickening of the executive core and capacities of the Assembly. And such, in terms of constitution building, is the long march through policy development, formulation and implementation.

The construction of the Executive Board

A closely related strand represents the most recent development: the construction of an Executive Board in place of the old-style Management Board for civil servants inherited from the Welsh Office (NAW, 2001). At one and the same time, this has gone virtually unremarked, and is a significant feature – being explicitly designed to strengthen internal co-ordination and the corporate focus of the Assembly's administrative branch. It may even prove the harbinger of a distinctive Welsh public service.

The new body is roughly double in size, boasting the eighteen or so most senior civil servants in the Assembly. And it has more expansive functions, including advice to the Permanent Secretary on input to cabinet, and managing the delivery of the priorities and targets in the administration's multiple strategic and operational plans. Once again, this is not the model of 'Welsh Office plus'. The Executive Board stands for a more solid core than was demanded in the old essentially administrative department.

In the words of the official documentation, 'the new board must . . . give clear leadership and direction to the staff.' It must 'build closer links with Cabinet, providing stronger collective support . . . be proactive and forward looking, not simply reacting to events . . . focus on delivering results and performance . . . address the management of policy as well as resources' (NAW, 2001). Turning the argument round, if official confirmation is needed that all has not been well in the administrative machine then this is it.

As so often in the short life of the Assembly, necessity is the mother of invention. The catalyst for change was a peer review of the effectiveness of the administration's business planning process (National Assembly Peer Review, 2001). A civil service organization 'under a degree of pressure' was the not so surprising conclusion, but one which served to underwrite calls for both a clearer definition of the role of senior staff and leadership from managers. In conjunction, that is, with the need to grow the capacity for policy development and for thinking about where the organization 'is and where it could be going'. Put simply, the elite 'top of the Office' was not to be spared the more bracing devolutionary air.

In fact, the scale of the institutional infilling is greater than at first appears. The Executive Board is at the apex of a new pyramidal structure or system of official committees. These include a business planning and delivery committee and a policy committee responsible for advising on and monitoring the management of policy development across the fields of devolved administration. The tentacles of the Executive Board are thus spread far and wide, and down into those motors of territorial government, the individual policy divisions.

This is not to overlook the genuine difficulties of promoting cultural change in the civil service (or anywhere else) (Laffin, 2002). The proof of this particular pudding will be firmly in the eating. The Permanent

Secretary, however, has set out his store. Perhaps, hopefully, the Executive Board will prove far more than a rotation of chairs.

CONCLUSION: A VIRTUAL PARLIAMENT

Confused and contested legal and constitutional framework, policy and politics in a novel devolutionary setting, public administration in the shadow of the (old) central government model: it was a recipe for internal difficulties. Clearly, however, the architects of the scheme could not reasonably have foreseen the crisis that engulfed the Assembly under Alun Michael, at least in terms of the speed and intensity. The shock waves have continued to reverberate. This is certainly not an example of the smooth path of devolution by evolution.

That its two main poles of authority have grown in stature is of the essence of the constitutional trajectory of the Assembly. Lord Elis-Thomas and his confrères have succeeded in establishing a strong measure of operational autonomy for the Presiding Office. Self-evidently, this too had not been anticipated, and it has created a different dynamic inside the Assembly. Meanwhile, the system of cabinet government has increasingly prospered under the coalition. The (Welsh) doctrine of collective responsibility, as well the attempts to inculcate a more proactive and strategic approach to territorial government and administration, epitomize this.

Special emphasis has been laid in this lecture on developments away from the public gaze, the tectonics of institutional and administrative change. The construction of the Executive Board, for example, is the more notable for having happened in silence. Whisper this gently: it is officials who can claim much of the credit for driving forward the devolutionary 'project'. Speaking more generally, the building blocks of a mature Welsh polity are increasingly in evidence, a phenomenon that reflects and reinforces an autochthonous constitutional development, howsoever dimly perceived.

As for the competing constitutional models, the first face – 'Welsh Office plus' – was largely disfigured by the fall of Alun Michael. In paradoxical fashion, the same fate befell the second face or strong corporate and collaborative model. Increasingly, it is the features of the third or parliamentary face – a de facto separation of powers – that have been accentuated, which in comparative constitutional perspective represents a flattening of differences. And, to reiterate, for those with the strategic vision this appeals as enhancing the prospect of a Parliament for Wales.

The theme can be pursued in several directions. First, the pull or attraction of 'Welsh Office plus' could be expected to fade over time. The key point is the element of acceleration. Second, the original design may be said to have underrated the 'background theory' of the British Constitution, in the sense of the mindset or deep values associated with an exceptionally strong tradition of parliamentary government (Craig, 1990). In the event, the contest between standard constitutional understandings, as expressed in the preference for separate roles and functions, and what I have called the extravagant version of the body corporate has proved to be an uneven one. Third, it is the way in which the different faces rub up one against each other that helps to explain many of the tensions or frictions. Better to convey the cross-currents of continuity and change, as also the sense of multifaceted and multilevel developments; let us now conceive of devolution not simply as a process, still less as an event, but as involving a series of processes that are more or less closely linked and elaborated. To repeat, devolution (to Wales) is so much more than the transference of powers.

A move to legislative devolution obviously is a political question, one on which the people of Wales would need to be consulted, including perhaps in a referendum. Such a question, however, is not asked in the abstract. The developments outlined in this lecture can once again be seen to have a broader significance: not only as helping to equip the (reinvented) devolved administration in case the answer is positive, but also as facilitating the putting of the question.

An interim constitution: this I suggest is how future O'Donnell Lecturers will view the current Welsh dispensation. But there is more to this idea than the negative sense generally conveyed of a lack of constitutional stability and excessive fragmentation of powers associated with the scheme of executive devolution. The lecture has directed attention to the more positive dimension of a framework for organic change, a not unfamiliar concept in comparative politics. Once again, this is not to commend the often tedious path of legal and institutional development that has been chosen, the nostrum of 'a process not an event' itself being a convenient disguise for many failings. There was much to be said for going direct to a form of legislative devolution (or indeed for never starting). But that is another story. Wales – the Assembly – is where it is.

Perhaps it is the nomenclature that best conveys the flavour. A presiding office, not OPO; ministers not Assembly secretaries; a cabinet not an executive committee; an Executive Board not a management board; and now the Welsh Assembly Government: one does not have to be a French philosopher to appreciate the symbolism of the change in language.[12] The National Assembly – a virtual parliament: such is the condition of Wales.

NOTES

1. As distinct from the legal name of the corporate body (the National Assembly for Wales): see further, *Official Record*, 8 January 2002 and 12 February 2002 (Presiding Officer's rulings).
2. In the guise of HM Treasury support for European Union structural funding for West Wales and the Valleys.
3. In the immediate aftermath of the change of first minister: see *Official Record*, 29 February 2000.
4. Office of the Presiding Officer, *Corporate Plan 1999/2000*, paragraph 3, id., *Corporate Plan 2000/2001*, paragraph 2.
5. Scotland Act 1998, s.21 and Schedule 2. See also B. Winetrobe, *Realising the Vision: A Parliament with a Purpose*, Constitution Unit, 2001.
6. House of Commons Debates, 25 March 1998, col. 562.
7. Made available on the Assembly cabinet website.
8. *Protocol*, made available on the Assembly cabinet website, paragraph 1.7.
9. This is not to overlook the absence by reason of police investigation of the leader of the Welsh Liberal Democrats, Michael German. For the latest cabinet reshuffle, see *Official Record*, 26 February 2002. Mr German has resumed office since the O'Donnell Lecture was delivered – Ed.
10. *Assembly Cabinet Minutes*, 3 December 2001.
11. As first established in May 2001, the system comprised subcommittees on children and young people, Corus, sustainable development and Wales in the world.
12. That is from the original terminology including in the statute (see especially GWA, Ch. 38, 1998, ss. 53, 56). Alternatively, for the visually inclined, reference may be made to the distinctive logo of the 'Welsh Assembly Government', officially unveiled on St David's Day 2002.

REFERENCES

Bogdanor, V. (ed.) (1991). *The Blackwell Encyclopaedia of Political Science*.
Chaney, P. and Fevre, R. (2001). 'Ron Davies and the cult of "inclusiveness": devolution and Participation in Wales', *Contemporary Wales*, 14, 131.
Cole, A. and Storer, A. (2002). 'Political dynamics in the Assembly: an emerging policy community', in Jones, J. B. and Balsom, D. (eds) (2002), *Building a Civic Culture*, Cardiff, Institute of Welsh Affairs.
Craig, P. (1990). *Public Law and Democracy in the United Kingdom and the United States of America*, Oxford, Clarendon.
Davies, G. P. (2000). *The National Assembly: The Year of Laying the Foundations*, Law Society of Wales.
Davies, R. (2000). 'We need a coalition of ideas', *Journal of the Institute of Welsh Affairs*, 27.
Davies, R. (1999). *Devolution: A Process not an Event*, Cardiff, Institute of Welsh Affairs.

Elis-Thomas, D. (2000). 'The first day of devolution'. *Western Mail*, 10 February.
Elis-Thomas, D. (2001a). 'The National Assembly: a year in power?', *Contemporary Wales*, 14, 50–6.
Elis-Thomas, D. (2001b). *Reviewing a Democratic Body*, Cardiff, Institute of Welsh Affairs.
Goldenberg, P. (1999). 'The Scottish coalition agreement', *Amicus Curiae*, 20, 4.
Government of Wales Act (GWA), Chapter 38 (1998). s.62.
Government of Wales Act (GWA), Chapter 38 (1998). s.1(2).
Government of Wales Act (GWA), Chapter 38 (1998). ss.53, 56–7.
Government of Wales Act (GWA), Chapter 38 (1998). s.34.
Jones, I. W. (2001). *From Assembly to Parliament*, Aberystwyth, Institute of Welsh Politics.
Jones, J. B. and Balsom, D. (eds) (2000). *The Road to the National Assembly for Wales*, Cardiff, University of Wales Press.
Jones, J. B. and Osmond, J. (2001). *Inclusive Government and Party Management*, Cardiff, Institute of Welsh Affairs.
Jones, J. B. and Osmond, J. (eds) (2002). *Building a Civic Culture*, Cardiff, Institute of Welsh Affairs.
Laffin, M. (2002). 'The engine room', in Jones, J. B. and Balsom, D. (eds), *Building a Civic Culture*, Cardiff, Institute of Welsh Affairs.
Laffin, M. (2001). 'Beyond Westminster', *Public Money and Management*, 21, 2.
Lambert, D. (2001). 'A voice for Wales: the National Assembly for Wales', in T. Watkin (ed.), *Legal Wales: Its Past, Its Future*, Welsh Legal History Society.
MacAllister, L. (2000). 'The new politics in Wales; rhetoric or reality', 53 *Parliamentary Affairs*, 591.
Marinetto, M. (2001). 'The settlement and process of devolution: territorial politics and governance under the Welsh Assembly', *Political Studies*, 49, 306.
Michael, A. (1999). *The Dragon on our Doorstep: New Politics for a New Millennium in Wales*, Aberystwyth, Institute of Welsh Politics.
Morgan, Rh. (2000). *Check against Delivery*, Aberystwyth, Institute of Welsh Politics.
Morgan, K. and Mungham, G. (2000). *Redesigning Democracy*, Bridgend, Seren.
National Assembly Advisory Group (NAAG) (1998). *National Assembly for Wales – A Consultation Paper*.
National Assembly for Wales (NAW) (1999). Transfer of Functions Order, SI 672.
National Assembly for Wales (NAW) (2000a). *Assembly Cabinet Minutes*, 13 March.
National Assembly for Wales (NAW) (2000b). *Arrangements for Making the Office of the Presiding Officer More Independent*, September.
National Assembly for Wales (NAW) (2001). *Transforming the Management Board*.
National Assembly for Wales (NAW) (2002a). *Assembly Review of Procedure*, February.
National Assembly for Wales (NAW) (2002b). *Official Record*, 14 February.
National Assembly Peer Review (2001). *Looking for the Route Map*.
Osmond, J. (2002). 'Constitution building on the hoof: the Assembly's procedural review', in Jones, J. B. and Osmond, J. (eds) (2002), *Building a Civic Culture*, Cardiff, Institute of Welsh Affairs.
Patchett, K. (2000). 'The new Welsh constitution: the Government of Wales Act

1998', in Jones, J. B. and Balsom, D. (eds), *The Road to the National Assembly for Wales*, Cardiff, University of Wales Press.

Rawlings, R. (forthcoming). *Delineating Wales: Legal and Constitutional Aspects of National Devolution*, Cardiff, University of Wales Press.

Rawlings, R. (2001). 'Quasi-legislative devolution: powers and principles', *Northern Ireland Legal Quarterly*, 54.

Rawlings, R. (1998). 'The new model Wales', *Journal of Law and Society*, 25, 461.

Robertson, D. (1993). *Dictionary of Politics*, 2nd edn, Penguin, 135.

Roddick, W. (1999). *Crossing the Road*, Law Society of Wales.

Scottish Labour Party and Scottish Liberal Democrats (1999). *The Scottish Coalition Agreement*.

Sherlock, A. (2000). 'Born free but everywhere in chains? A legal analysis of the first year of the National Assembly for Wales', *Cambrian Law Review*, 31, 59.

Storer, A. and Lang, M. (2001). *Institutional Evolution: The Operation of the Welsh Executive*, Cardiff, Welsh Governance Centre, Working Paper No. 5.

Welsh Labour Party (1997). *Representing Wales*.

Welsh Labour Party and Welsh Liberal Democrats (2000). *Putting Wales First: A Partnership for the People of Wales*, October.

Williams, D. (1999). 'The devolution of powers from central government', in Miers, D. (ed.), *Devolution in Wales: Public Law and the National Assembly*, Wales Public Law and Human Rights Association.

2. HOW OBJECTIVE 1 ARRIVED IN WALES: THE POLITICAL ORIGINS OF A COUP

Kevin Morgan

THE FALL AND RISE OF OBJECTIVE 1 STATUS

Like a shimmering but elusive trophy, awarded for regional failure, Objective 1 status had exercised local authorities in Wales long before it became a formal reality in March 1999. One of the most exercised of all in this respect was Mid Glamorgan County Council, which bizarrely had its headquarters in Cardiff even though it embraced the central valleys, one of the most socially deprived areas in the entire UK. As the economic centre of gravity in south Wales edged slowly but surely from the coalfield to the coast, the valley communities saw themselves enmeshed in an increasingly schizophrenic relationship with Cardiff and its hinterland. On the one hand, the region's labour markets were becoming ever more integrated, with over a third of Cardiff's workforce migrating daily to the city from the valleys, reversing the original pattern of economic dependence which had grown up when coal was king, when the city was subordinate to the coalfield. On the other hand, the coalfield communities resented the fact that they were locked into Cardiff and South Glamorgan for European Union (EU) administrative purposes, the whole sub-region being part of the southern NUTS 2 region when the Structural Funds were reformed in 1988.[1]

Because a Tory-managed Welsh Office had little or no interest in exploring the case for Objective 1 status, this task fell to the local authorities, especially Mid Glamorgan, which had most to gain from a programme designed to regenerate the poorest areas of the European Union. But, time and again, the best efforts of local politicians and officers were dashed by the geopolitics of a north–south map which aggregated the coalfield with the coast, with the result that the poverty of the former was rendered 'invisible' by the prosperity of the latter. Mid Glamorgan argued that the whole valleys should be classified on their own, in which case they would most certainly have passed the one and only statistical test for Objective 1 status – namely a GDP per capita of less than 75 per cent of the EU average.

Unfortunately this case never managed to surmount the complex bureaucratic hurdles, not the least of which was the claim that the population of the valleys was too small for it to constitute a NUTS 2 region on its own. Far more important, though, was the fact that there was no political will to fight the case on behalf of the valleys, or any other part of Wales for that matter, in a Tory-managed Welsh Office which was content to administer the status quo.

In retrospect, one can say that the 1997 election transformed the situation because, with the advent of the Ron Davies team, the Welsh Office became a bolder and more proactive government department (Morgan and Mungham, 2000). Among the priorities of the Labour-controlled Welsh Office none was deemed to be more important than the goal of securing Objective 1 regeneration funds for the poorest parts of Wales.

THE BATTLE OF THE MAPS: NORTH–SOUTH VERSUS WEST–EAST

The campaign to secure Objective 1 status for Wales was aided and abetted by two totally unrelated factors. Firstly, as we have seen, there was a new political resolve to mount a robust campaign, a factor that had been totally absent in the past. Secondly, and perhaps more important, the existing regulations governing the Structural Funds were due to expire on 31 December 1999 and a new generation of Objective 1 areas had to be agreed on or before the Berlin summit of EU leaders in March 1999. In other words, what we had here was a unique confluence of political leadership and historical opportunity.

Over the summer of 1998 the Welsh Office team – led by Ron Davies, Peter Hain and Wyn Griffiths on the political side and Rachel Lomax, the dynamic new permanent secretary, on the civil service side – began pressing the Welsh case for Objective 1 status with the Treasury. This effort was very much a private affair, not least because Ron Davies did not want to embarrass, still less, alienate the new chancellor by mounting a public campaign before the idea had been properly 'flagged up' behind closed doors. On the other hand, he realized that there had to be a public campaign to complement his discreet administrative campaign, otherwise Treasury mandarins could very easily squander the opportunity through inaction –

and everyone was painfully aware that the December 1999 deadline for the Structural Funds was fast approaching. Everyone involved in the campaign recognized that the Objective 1 case revolved around the legitimacy of a new NUTS 2 map of Wales, a map which substituted a west–east division of Wales for the old north–south division. It was at this point, during the summer of 1998, that I became personally involved in the campaign.

By way of context, I should perhaps say that, during his period in opposition, Ron Davies had asked me to convene an academic think-tank which he could use as a 'sounding board' for new policy initiatives should Labour win power at the next election. This informal (and unpaid) arrangement worked reasonably well, so much so that it evolved into a strong political relationship based on mutual trust. This was the personal background against which I received a phone call from him at the Welsh Office in which he had two things to say: (i) the case for Objective 1 status was precariously balanced and it was impossible to call; and (ii) it was essential to mount a public case for a new east–west map, a case which came from civil society rather than the Welsh Office because this was felt to have more influence in the corridors of power in London and Brussels. If I agreed to make a case for the new map, his contribution would be to get his officials to supply all the necessary data and to arrange for the Institute of Welsh Affairs to publish it. For the public record, I should also say that my reward for undertaking the task would take the form of 'psychic income', as the Secretary of State felicitously put it. The key message he wanted to convey, however, was that the battle for Objective 1 status would be won or lost on the issue of the east–west map being acceptable to the Office for National Statistics and Eurostat, the statistical bureaucracies in London and Brussels.

I agreed to drop everything and do the work simply because I believed that without an east–west map there would be no Objective 1 programme in Wales in the new round of the Structural Funds. That was the primary consideration in my mind and it overrode any lingering doubts I might have entertained about accepting the task – like the doubts about being party to a gerrymandering exercise, for example. (Academia is perhaps one of the few occupations in which one can engage in this kind of intellectual self-indulgence: indeed, for most people there would be no ethical conflict as to whether one should participate in an exercise which could bring over £1 billion of regeneration funds to the most deprived areas of the country.) In the event, I asked Adam Price, at that time the director of research at Menter a Busnes and my former research assistant, to undertake the task with me because it was too much work in too short a time for me to do alone.

The report that we eventually produced was called *The Other Wales*, a title designed to highlight the plight of what we called the 'forgotten communities' of the west and the valleys (Morgan and Price, 1998). The introduction to the report tried to address the problem of maps in general, and particularly the role they play in revealing and concealing certain underlying realities. The introduction opened with the following paragraphs, perhaps the best way to illustrate the problem as we saw it at the time:

We live in a paradoxical world in which information overload co-exists with ever-growing uncertainty and complexity. To help us make sense of this world we all carry mental maps in our heads which help us form opinions, make decisions and design strategies for coping with a reality where the only constant is change. But our mental maps can sometimes outlast the reality which generated them in the first place, in which case they become not aids but barriers to understanding, preventing us from recognising new patterns, trends and configurations. This problem is especially acute in the sphere of economic geography, where, for example, localities and regions strive, through 'place-marketing' strategies, to present stylised pictures of their areas in the hope of attracting mobile capital investment. It is not that these pictures are wholly false but, rather, that they are highly filtered expressions of a more diverse, more complex reality: they extol growth over decline, the positive over the negative and, because of this, they flatter to deceive.

The central contention of this report is that a particular mental map of Wales has been constructed in recent years which has been so successfully marketed by the WDA, in conjunction with successive governments, that it threatens to be counter-productive in the context of the imminent reforms of EU Structural Funds on the one hand and the UK Assisted Areas on the other. This mental map – of a Wales which has successfully negotiated the transition from coal and steel to a diversified economy based on manufacturing and services – conceals as much as it reveals, not least because it suggests that Wales has overcome its traditional economic problems, when it manifestly has not.

The successes which figure prominently in the WDA's mental map refer not to Wales as a whole but to certain regions within Wales, principally to south east Wales and to north east Wales, the two most buoyant regions of the Welsh economy. The main regional division in Wales today is not the traditional division between south Wales and the Rest (the division which is enshrined in Eurostat's NUTS 2 classification of Wales) but between west and east. In this report we aim to show that this west/east division, which contains economic, social, and even political dimensions, has been rendered 'invisible' to politicians and policy-makers partly because our traditional mental maps, aided and abetted by existing, but outmoded, EU statistical classifications, are attuned to a different division, the north/south division'.

Although we were manifestly engaged in a *political* enterprise – redrawing a map so as to access EU regeneration funds – we were surprised by the extent to which the social and economic indicators really did suggest that a plausible intellectual case could be made along these lines. Of course, the west–east division underplayed the pockets of acute deprivation in the east, notably the deprived wards which coexisted, cheek by jowl, with the leafier parts of the capital city (Morgan and Price, 1992). But on a whole series of indicators – unemployment, inactivity, limiting long-term illness, earnings and GDP, for example – we concluded that a robust case could indeed be made for saying that a west–east division was rooted in the reality of contemporary Wales.

There was another challenge apart from the production of a new NUTS 2 map, and that was whether the GDP per capita of the new western region was lower than 75 per cent of the EU average, the statistical acid test to qualify for Objective 1. In retrospect this might seem to be a simple technical matter, in the sense that the figure was either above or below this critical threshold. At the time, however, the issue was fraught with many imponderables – the most important being, firstly, which methodology to use for the GDP per capita calculations and, secondly, whether or not to include Conwy and Denbighshire in the western NUTS 2 region (that is, in the proposed Objective 1 region).

In our report we surveyed the different methodologies that were being used at the time to calculate GDP per capita figures, including the 'workplace-based' methodology which was being used by ONS and Eurostat. What further compounded the problem was that, at the time, there were no official data for GDP per capita for unitary authorities in Wales. The House of Commons Library presented a workplace-based analysis and concluded that thirteen Welsh unitary authorities, all of them in the western and valleys region, had a GDP per capita below 75 per cent of the EU average, and many of them were well below it.

Further uncertainty was injected into the calculations by the issue of which unitary authorities should be included. One school of thought argued that Conwy and Denbighshire should not be included because their GDP per capita levels were dangerously close to the 75 per cent threshold, and if employment-based estimates were used they actually exceeded the threshold.

The alternative school argued that these northern authorities should be included for the sake of inclusivity in post-devolution Wales, in other words, to send a signal to the north that its interests would not be ignored by a Labour-controlled administration in Cardiff. In the event, the two northern counties were included in the Objective 1 region – not as a result of a technical statistical exercise, but because Ron Davies took a political gamble to do so.

Throughout this period, the signals coming from the Treasury were anything but reassuring. The Welsh Office's private campaign to persuade the key Whitehall department of the merits of their case was meeting resistance. The Treasury was uncomfortable with many aspects of the case, especially the scale of the proposed Objective 1 region, which if successful would embrace some two-thirds of the entire population of Wales. Treasury officials were also suggesting that Wales did not meet all the technical criteria and this in turn would make it difficult, if not impossible, for ONS to convince Eurostat of the merits of the case.

Behind the scenes, however, the private political campaign was gaining momentum. Tony Blair was persuaded to raise the case directly with Jacques Santer, the European Commission president. Ron Davies and Peter Hain shuttled between Cardiff and Brussels to press their case directly with Monika Wulf-Mathies, the EU Commissioner for Regional Policy. And of course Neil Kinnock, at that time the EU Transport Commissioner, was pressing the case from within the European Commission. The intensity of this behind-the-scenes political campaign was camouflaged by Neil Kinnock, who told the *Western Mail* that 'it is an entirely statistical battle' (Hornung, 2000).

However, the political campaign for Objective 1 status was not entirely a private, behind-the-scenes affair. As regards the public campaign, Dafydd Wigley, the Plaid Cymru leader, was second to none in promoting the Welsh case. Whenever the Welsh Office seemed to be dragging its feet on the Objective 1 issue, Wigley was on hand to provide a judicious mixture of criticism and support. In a high-profile speech in May 1998, he argued that the west–east divide was now accepted by politicians of every persuasion; even so, he estimated that the chances of securing Objective 1 status were at best evens (Wigley, 1998).

Shortly before our report, *The Other Wales*, went to press, the government announced that an agreement had been reached with Eurostat on a revised NUTS classification. As regards Wales, the statement simply said: 'the two-way split of Wales to be on an East/West basis, rather than the current

North/South structure. This reflects the evolving differences between the East and the less accessible Western and Valleys areas.' Encouraging as it was, this statement did not guarantee that the Objective 1 case had been won because the critical GDP per capita figure for the western region had still not been officially calculated. Indeed, it was not until October 1998 that ONS officially announced that the western region had passed the eligibility test for Objective 1 status. The crescent shaped western region – running from Denbighshire in the north, through Gwynedd, Ceredigion and Carmarthenshire, to Torfaen in the south – had been officially accepted as having a GDP per capita of 73 per cent on 1996 figures, thus meeting the EU test with just 2 per cent to spare.

With the exception of the 1997 devolution referendum, another close-run thing, this was Ron Davies's biggest political coup as Secretary of State for Wales. More importantly, it was a major achievement for a broadly based campaign to have overcome the initial hostility of the Treasury, and the debilitating scepticism of some Welsh Office mandarins who thought it too ambitious or else too troublesome. Most important of all, though, it offered a unique opportunity for the most deprived parts of Wales to realize their unpretentious hopes of a better future.

The battle for Objective 1 status for West Wales and the Valleys had effectively been won by October 1998, even though the official historians will say that Tony Blair secured the victory at the Berlin Summit in March 1999, when the EU leaders agreed the financial framework for the 2000–6 period. Strictly speaking, the Berlin Summit agreed the financial sums which were attached to Objective 1 rather than the question of which regions were eligible. Nevertheless, this did not stop Tony Blair returning to a hero's reception at the Welsh Labour Party conference at Llandudno, where he presented himself as the man who brought Objective 1 to Wales. The Objective 1 package was certainly formalized in Berlin in March 1999, and to that extent the Prime Minister was centrally involved. But for all intents and purposes the battle had ended in victory six months earlier, a testament to the power of collective and focused action.

THE WAR IS OVER, BEWARE OF THE PEACE

The Brechtian slogan 'the war is over, beware of the peace' was meant to be a plea for eternal vigilance, an injunction not to rest on one's laurels after a demanding campaign. Oddly enough, this was the key message from Graham Meadows, a senior Brussels official, when he addressed the

Euro-community in Wales at the Copthorne Hotel in Cardiff in January 1999. Well-known to the Welsh Euro-community, Meadows was also widely liked and respected, not least because he brought a frank and unpretentious attitude to his work. Above all, though, he made time to listen. Because he rarely spoke from a formal script, I noted the key points he made at the time because they distilled good practice from around the EU. Of the many important messages he conveyed that day, I want to highlight two of them here because they are essential to the success of the Objective 1 programme:

- To waste no time in building real as opposed to formal partnerships: keep meeting each other because this helps to build up the trust that is necessary to exchange information and to bind the enterprise.
- To recognize that securing Objective 1 status was the easy part, whereas the hard part was to spend it wisely and effectively. This was especially important in Wales, he said bluntly, because the Objective 2 programme in industrial South Wales in the 1990s had exposed some very serious question marks about the local capacity to make the most of EU funds.

Something went wrong between the sound advice that was on offer at the Copthorne Hotel in January and December, when the Welsh Objective 1 plan (the Single Programming Document) was savaged by the European Commission because its weaknesses were 'more comprehensive than the strengths'. I have examined what went wrong in detail elsewhere (Morgan, 2000), so I do not want to repeat it here. Suffice it to say that the Objective 1 process fell victim to a whole series of political problems, not least the debilitating Alun Michael affair, the perennial arguments over match-funding and the more systemic problem of the Assembly's being overworked and under-resourced.

The Objective 1 match-funding issue may have triggered the downfall of Alun Michael, but it was certainly not the key factor – the underlying cause has to be sought in his command-and-control style of leadership. The match-funding deal which Gordon Brown announced in July 2000, as part of the Comprehensive Spending Review, came too late to save the first First Minister. Although only time will tell whether sufficient match funding will be available over the full course of the Objective 1 programme, there is no doubt that the Chancellor made some significant revisions to the population-based Barnett formula to enable Wales to access Objective 1 funds (Bristow, 2001).

Will the Objective 1 programme really make a difference to the quality of life in West Wales and the Valleys? Sadly, we will not know the answer to this question for some time to come, when many of the politicians and officers in charge today may no longer be around to enjoy the acclaim or shoulder the blame. The current regulations governing the Structural Funds are more demanding and more draconian than all previous regulations because they contain a 'decommitment' clause. This is an inelegant euphemism for the fact that the European Commission is entitled to claw back any money that is not spent within two years of the year in which it was committed. In other words this clause sets a high premium on timely and effective management structures, high-calibre partnerships and well-defined projects.

At the moment, it is impossible to say whether we are up to the task of making a success of Objective 1 status. The scale of the programme means that it is a steep learning curve for everyone involved and the skills necessary to make it a success are not easily acquired. Indeed, the most recent independent evidence we have says quite bluntly that the Welsh European Funding Office (WEFO) 'has had difficulty since its inception in recruiting sufficient staff with the right skills' (Auditor General for Wales, 2002).

From our limited experience to date, we can say that one of the most important skills of all is a facility to be self-critical, to be able to monitor and evaluate work in progress and to accommodate constructive criticism of the process. In short, problems cannot be redressed if there is a refusal to acknowledge them in the first place. A mature political culture can accommodate constructive criticism because it is perceived to be part of the process of collective learning and incremental innovation. One of the dangers facing the Objective 1 programme, and the Assembly more generally, is the tendency to misconstrue constructive criticism as 'talking Wales down', a tendency which fosters loyalty for its own sake and which is ultimately the kiss of death for democracy and development alike. For this reason, the fate of the Objective 1 programme will be a barometer of our political culture as well as a measure of our economic capacity.

NOTES

1. The Nomenclature of Territorial Units for Statistics (NUTS) was established by Eurostat to provide a single uniform breakdown of territorial units for the production of regional statistics for the EU. The original NUTS system was a five-level hierarchical classification of three regional levels and two local levels. For example, Wales is equivalent to a NUTS 1 level unit and groups of counties constitute a NUTS 2 level unit (see ONS, 1996).

REFERENCES

Auditor General for Wales (2002). *EU Structural Funds: Maximising the Benefits for Wales*, Cardiff, National Audit Office Wales.

Bristow, G. (2001). 'Bypassing Barnett: the comprehensive spending review and public expenditure in Wales', *Economic Affairs*, September.

Hornung, R. (2000). 'How an east–west split won the battle in Berlin', *Western Mail*, Objective 1 Survey, 19 January.

Morgan, K and Price, A. (1992). *Rebuilding Our Communities: A New Agenda for the Valleys*, Friedrich Ebert Foundation.

Morgan, K. and Price, A. (1998). *The Other Wales: The Case for Objective 1 Funding Post 1999*, Cardiff, Institute of Welsh Affairs.

Morgan, K. and Mungham, G. (2000). *Redesigning Democracy: The Making of the Welsh Assembly*, Bridgend, Seren.

Morgan, K. (2000). 'The two worlds of Objective One', *Agenda: Journal of the Institute of Welsh Affairs*, Summer.

Office for National Statistics (ONS) (1996). *Draft Proposals for the Nomenclature of Territorial Units (NUTS): The Classification of Areas for European Purposes*, London, ONS.

Wigley, D. (1998). *Wales and the European Monetary Union*, Welsh Business Lecture, Cardiff International Arena, 15 May.

3. OBJECTIVE 1: A COMPARATIVE ASSESSMENT

John Bachtler

INTRODUCTION

The Objective 1 programme for West Wales and the Valleys is one of seven Objective 1 programmes in the UK, involving a total cost of some €14.4 billion (*c.* £8.8 billion) and accounting for almost 30 per cent of UK receipts under Objective 1 of the Structural Funds for the period 2000–6. Almost three years into the new programme period, it is an opportune moment to reflect on the launch and implementation of the UK Objective 1 programmes and to put the experiences of the West Wales and the Valleys programme into a wider context. Across the UK, the Objective 1 programmes are being implemented in very different institutional contexts and with varying administrative arrangements, the common experience being one of a complex and challenging programming environment.

This article examines the progress of the new generation of UK Objective 1 programmes to date and the challenges that lie ahead. It begins by outlining the basic details of the programmes – expenditure, strategic objectives, priorities – and compares the different implementation arrangements through which they are being delivered. The article then examines the current and future management problems faced in the present period, before concluding with a discussion of the future of the Structural Funds from a UK perspective.

OBJECTIVE 1 PROGRAMMES IN THE UK

West Wales and the Valleys is one of four fully eligible UK Objective 1 regions receiving structural fund assistance for the period 2000–6, the other three being Merseyside, South Yorkshire and Cornwall and the Isles of

Scilly. In addition, there are two formerly eligible Objective 1 regions with transitional programmes – Highlands and Islands and Northern Ireland – providing Structural Fund on a degressive basis for a six-year period (2000–5). Lastly, there is a multi-regional Objective 1 programme in Northern Ireland for 'Peace and reconciliation' (Peace II), operated jointly with the Republic of Ireland.

Strategic orientations
In Wales and elsewhere, the common feature of all of the UK Objective 1 programmes is an attempted transformation of economic-development performance and prospects. There is a strong focus on sustainability, defined variously in economic and environmental terms, and on individuals and communities. Many have strategic aims (see Table 3.1) using strong motivational and aspirational language, for example, a 'world class city region' (Merseyside) or 'putting people first' (West Wales and the Valleys). The strategic objectives primarily address job creation, skill enhancement, business performance, social exclusion and the environment.

These strategic orientations have been influenced by several factors. First, during the preparation of the programmes, there was more extensive consultation with partners than in previous programme periods. The delivery of Structural Funds over the past twelve to fifteen years has created a large community of increasingly well-informed partners. This consultation was supported by more thorough analysis of regional strategic needs and interim/*ex-post* evaluation of previous programmes, as well as greater political scrutiny resulting from devolution in Wales, Scotland and Northern Ireland. Second, the Structural Funds were very specific about what the Single Programming Documents (SPDs) needed to contain and the processes by which they should be drawn up. The European Commission provided clearer guidance (CEC, 1999) on its thematic and horizontal priorities for the new programmes and it worked closely with many regions in a more interactive process of programme development. Third, there was a widespread and universal commitment among programme management authorities to maximize the opportunities of this (potentially) last period of Structural Fund support and to leave a 'durable legacy'.

Despite the big differences in the size, location, problems and institutional contexts of the Objective 1 regions, there is a broadly standard response in terms of priorities for intervention. Reflecting the influence of the European Commission's guidance, the priorities are mainly concerned with five issues (CEC, 2001):

TABLE 3.1
Strategic aims and priorities of the UK Objective 1 programmes

Strategic aims	Priorities
West Wales and the Valleys Putting 'people first' through developing skills and attitudes to allow the region to compete as a modern advanced economy and to develop an entrepreneurial spirit in all sectors of the economy and society.	• Developing SME base • Innovation and the knowledge economy • Community economic regeneration • Developing people • Rural development and sustainable resources • Strategic infrastructure development
Merseyside A world-class city region that attracts people to live, work and invest.	• Developing business • Developing people • Developing locations • Developing pathways communities
South Yorkshire A balanced, diverse and sustainable high-growth economy, recognised as a growing European centre for high technology manufacturing and knowledge based services, and offering opportunities for the whole community.	• Stimulating new growth and high tech sectors • Competitiveness and innovation • Equity, employment and social inclusion • Economic opportunities in targeted communities • Strategic spatial development • Foundations for a successful programme
Cornwall and Scilly A step change in prosperity, making the region a place where people and communities have equal access to opportunities and to a quality of life which arises from the sustainable development of its economy and its environment and the enhancement of its distinctiveness.	• SME and micro-business support • Strategic investments • Developing people • Community economic development and rural adjustment • Regional distinctiveness
Highlands and Islands Prosperous self-sustaining communities where the unique cultures, traditions and environments are enhanced and the region makes a distinctive contribution to Scotland, the UK and the EU.	• Increasing business competitiveness • Creating the conditions for regional competitiveness • Developing the region's human resources • Support for the primary sector and related food industry
Northern Ireland Moving Northern Ireland to a state of sustainable prosperity in a competitive and modern economy by focusing on the restructuring of its businesses and the key-skills development of its people while maintaining a quality environment.	• Economic growth and competitiveness • Employment • Urban and social revitalization • Agriculture, rural development, forestry and fisheries • Environment
Northern Ireland Peace II Reinforcing progress towards a peaceful and stable society and to promote reconciliation.	• Economic renewal • Social integration, inclusion and reconciliation • Locally-based regeneration and development strategies • Promoting an outward and forward-looking region • Cross-border co-operation

Source: SPDs and Inforegio website.

- the development of Small and Medium-Sized Enterprises (SMEs) through capital investment, business advice and training;
- community economic development/regeneration;
- human resource support (applying the European Employment Strategy);
- infrastructure development;
- rural economic diversification.

In the view of the European Commission, the outcomes were programmes considered to be of 'acceptable quality', with the exception of Cornwall and the Scilly Isles which was deemed to be of 'high quality' (CEC, 2001).

PROGRAMME RESOURCES

The West Wales and the Valleys programme (€1.85 billion) is the largest of the UK Objective 1 programmes, with 35 per cent of the total allocation, followed by Merseyside (€1.3 billion) and South Yorkshire (€1.1 billion). The UK Objective 1 programmes have been allocated Structural Funds of €6.5 billion (see Table 3.2), representing about five per cent of the EU's total Objective 1 budget. On a per capita basis, West Wales and the Valleys is receiving €993 per person in the eligible area, considerably higher than the UK average but somewhat less than Cornwall and the Isles of Scilly which is receiving the greatest allocation per capita. Taking account of the differing time periods over which the money will be spent, the differences between the fully eligible and transitional regions decreases – indeed, South Yorkshire is receiving less per head per year than the transitional Highlands and Islands programme – and all programmes have Structural Fund receipts in the range of €124–146 per person per year.

There are also some differences in the financial allocations within programmes (see Table 3.3). For example, European Regional Development Fund (ERDF) allocations are generally higher in the urban/industrial programme areas, associated with greater potential for spending on infrastructure and business support, while European Agricultural Guidance and Guarantee Fund (EAGGF)/Financial Instrument for Fisheries Guidance (FIFG) are only relevant to the rural/coastal programmes. For the UK as a whole, about 62 per cent of Objective 1 spending is allocated to ERDF, 31 percent to European Structural Fund (ESF), and the remaining 7 per cent to EAGGF and FIFG – a pattern that is almost identical to the breakdown for the West Wales and the Valleys programme. Among the other UK programmes, the main contrast (with the exception of Northern

TABLE 3.2

Financial allocations to UK Objective 1 programmes (2000–2006)

Region/programme	Structural funds allocation (€m)	Eligible population (million)	Structural funds per person (€)	Structural funds per person per year (€)
West Wales and Valleys	1,853	1.867	993	142
Merseyside	1,333	1.42	939	134
South Yorkshire	1,173	1.3	902	129
Cornwall and Scilly Isles	498	0.486	1025	146
Highlands & Islands	309	0.372	831	138
N. Ireland Transitional	891	1.690	527	88
N. Ireland Peace II	425	1.690	251	36
Total	6,481	7.135	908	130

TABLE 3.3

Breakdown of financial allocations to UK Objective 1 programmes (2000–2006)

Region/programme	Total cost	Structural funds				National aid[1]		Private sector[2]	
		Total	percentage allocations to:						
	€ m	€ m	ERDF	ESF	EAGGF	FIFG	€m	%	€m	%
West Wales & Valleys	3,937	1,853	60	32	7	1	1,392	43	692	18
Merseyside	3,298	1,333	67	33	0	0	1,333	50	631	19
South Yorkshire	3,039	1,173	67	31	2	0	1,103	48	764	25
Cornwall & Scilly Isles	1,181	498	60	20	16	3	483	49	200	17
Highlands & Islands	853	309	59	19	13	9	367	54	177	21
N. Ireland Transitional	1,514	891	57	31	9	3	447	33	177	12
N. Ireland Peace II	595	425	57	35	8	0	142	25	28	5
Total	14,417	6,481	62	31	6	1	5,267	46	2,669	19

Source: CEC (2001). Note: (1) National aid figures are for total national allocations and percentage of total public sector cost. (2) Private sector figures are for total private contributions and percentage of total programme cost.

Ireland) is between the urban programmes (Merseyside, South Yorkshire), which allocated some two-thirds of planned expenditure to ERDF measures, and the predominantly rural programmes (Highlands and Islands, Cornwall and Scilly Isles), where less than 60 per cent is allocated to ERDF and a further fifth to ESF and EAGGF/FIFG interventions respectively.

There are bigger contrasts in the shares of national assistance and the private sector within programmes, essentially reflecting the types of priorities/measures and regional judgements on the likely availability of match funding for different interventions and the possibility of attracting private sector contributions. With respect to national aid, the two Northern Ireland operational programmes have a very low national contribution – 25 per cent in the case of Peace II, 33 per cent in the case of the transitional programme – whereas, at the other extreme, the national contribution to the transitional Highlands and Islands is about 54 per cent. The private sector contribution ranges from 5 per cent of total programme costs in Peace II programme to 25 per cent in South Yorkshire, the private sector making a contribution of about one-sixth of expected programme expenditure across the UK as a whole.

IMPLEMENTING THE NEW PROGRAMMES

The distinctive feature of Structural Funds implementation in the UK is diversity. More so than other EU Member States, there are significant differences between the constituent parts of the UK in the way that Structural Fund programmes are managed and delivered. There have also been more change over time in the evolution of implementation structures than in most other countries.

In Wales, of course, the Objective 1, 2 and 3 programmes are administered by an executive agency of the National Assembly for Wales, the Welsh European Funding Office (WEFO), with operational delegation for implementing parts of the programme to regional and local partnerships. This system superseded the implementation arrangements for the 1994–9 period, when programme management responsibilities were delegated to the Welsh European Partnership Executive (WEPE), which in turn superseded the exclusive control of Structural Funds by the Welsh Office.

The approach in Wales has similarities with the implementation of Structural Funds in Northern Ireland where the management and delivery of EU funding is formally the responsibility of the Department of Finance and Personnel within the Northern Ireland Executive. In practice, administration is delegated to a mix of government departments, intermediary bodies and local partnerships, depending on the type of funding. Delegation applies, in particular, to the Peace II programme where 'local strategy partnerships' play an important role in programme delivery at district level.

In England, implementation of the Structural Funds was controlled totally by the regional Government Offices until the establishment of the Regional Development Agencies, which now lead on strategic issues, with the administration of the programme remaining in the Government Offices. At the start of the current programming period, there was some interest in 'decoupling' programme management from the Government Offices in the English regions. This was resisted, except in South Yorkshire where the Objective 1 management secretariat has been transferred away from the Government Office for Yorkshire and the Humber to an 'Objective 1 programme executive', established collectively by the GO-YH, the South Yorkshire Forum and the Yorkshire Forward regional development agency. Several English regions manage their programmes through delegated administrative arrangements, whereby aspects of project generation and selection have been transferred to sub-regional or thematic partnerships through 'packages' (for example, North-East England) or Action Plans (for example, North-West England, East Midlands).

Lastly, in Scotland, all of the Structural Fund programmes are managed through 'Programme Management Executives' (PMEs). These are separate organizations, operating under authority delegated from the Scottish Executive (which is the formal managing authority) to manage programmes on behalf of the regional partnerships in the Highlands and Islands, and the West, South and East of Scotland (and on behalf of the Objective 3 partnership). This 'Scottish model' was originally pioneered in the West of Scotland by the former Strathclyde Regional Council and has since been developed to apply across the country. Scotland is also the only part of the UK where there is effective operational networking across programme boundaries, through a 'Scottish Co-ordination Team' to promote information sharing and exchange of experience. A 'European Structural Fund Forum' has also been established to bring together ministers, members of the Scottish, Westminster and European parliaments, trade unions, universities and other bodies.

MANAGEMENT CHALLENGES

The UK Objective 1 programmes appear to making broadly similar progress in programme delivery, although at slightly different rates (see Table 3.4). Among those programmes for which comparable data are available, most have committed about one-quarter of programme resources (under one-fifth in the case of Merseyside), and have generally paid out grants of 5–9 per cent of the total budget (less than 4 per cent in the case of Cornwall and the Isles of Scilly). The first crucial test of progress will be on 31 December 2002 when all the programmes will be expected to have paid out expenditure for project

TABLE 4
Progress of UK Objective 1 Programmes

Objective 1 area	Number of projects	Committed grant		Grant paid	
		£ m	% of total	£ m	% of total
West Wales & the Valleys	441	152.0	26.40	68.2	5.98
South Yorkshire	192	198.2	27.96	48.5	6.84
Cornwall & Isles of Scilly	180	75.6	24.57	10.6	3.45
Merseyside	674	301.2	18.00	78.9	9.34

Source: House of Commons *Hansard*, written answer for 25 February 2002.

commitments made in the first year of operation, under the so-called 'N+2' rule. Failing that, expenditure not paid out on commitments made will be 'decommitted' or lost to the programmes. Like their Objective 2 counterparts, all of the Objective 1 programmes are finding this programming period to be a challenging management exercise, for several reasons.

First, there is greater pressure to ensure the timely commitment and expenditure of financial resource to avoid decommitment. This involves having monitoring mechanisms that can provide 'real time' information on the state of programme progress to monitoring committees, programme managers and partners, as well as ensuring that applicants and beneficiaries are aware of the need to implement projects and submit claims relatively quickly.

Second, the financial control regulations are stricter than previously. Projects are subject to multiple layers of audit, not just financial monitoring by the programme secretariat and evaluation but also audit by national authorities, different Commission services and the Court of Auditors. These controls are being exercised in different ways over different timescales and imposing a significant burden on programmes.

Third, the monitoring obligations are also more stringent. More so than in previous programming periods, programmes have been required to provide indicators and quantified targets for all interventions, against which progress will be assessed. The first assessment will be through the 'mid-term review' (interim evaluation) taking place in 2003, the results of which will be used to determine the allocation of the so-called 'performance reserve' (a tranche of funding held back by the Commission to be awarded in line with programme performance). While in England there will be competition between the Objective 1 programmes for this reserve, in Wales the competition will be between different parts of the programme.

Lastly, apart from the Commission requirements, most programmes have had to adapt to new management and administrative arrangements. Apart from the political and institutional changes associated with devolution and decentralization, many secretariats have introduced new programme implementation mechanisms involving (in some cases) 'decentralized arrangements' for project selection, new management information and monitoring systems, and rationalized administrative procedures to accelerate the processing of applications and claims.

REFLECTIONS

This brief review of Objective 1 programmes in the UK has provided a comparison of the West Wales and the Valleys programme with its counterparts in other parts of the UK. It indicates that the objectives, resource allocation and implementation structure of the Welsh Objective 1 programme are broadly similar to other UK programmes, and that its performance (in terms of commitment and payment levels) is in line with trends elsewhere.

What the comparative tables do not show, however, are the qualitative aspects of programming, such as the efficiency of programme management, the effectiveness of the new partnership structures and the quality of projects. It is evident from other articles in this volume, as well as political debate and media comment in Wales, that the launch and progress of the Objective 1 programme have not been easy and that there are controversies surrounding the management and delivery of the programme.

Making judgements from an external perspective is always risky, but there are several aspects of the current, difficult environment for the West Wales and the Valleys Objective 1 programme that are striking to an outsider. First, the division of Wales along west–east lines has created a totally new programme area, combining both urban/industrial and rural areas that were formerly part of separate programmes. No other Objective 1 region in the UK has this complex mix of regional development challenges. Second, the relative efficiency of Structural Fund implementation in some other parts of the UK is based on a history of learning over the past ten to fifteen years. In Wales, the creation and then abolition of WEPE and then creation of WEFO has inhibited continuity of learning and lost a significant part of the institutional experience accumulated in recent years.

Third, devolution has brought Structural Fund programmes under closer political scrutiny in Wales, Scotland and Northern Ireland, but Wales is distinctive in having politicians engaged in the actual implementation process. With the possible exception of Northern Ireland, no other UK programme experiences this degree of 'politicization' of the structural funds. Fourth, the changeover from Objective 2/5b to Objective 1 has been difficult, owing to the scale of additional funding, the greater complexity of the programme (in terms of the mix of funds and interventions) and the greater awareness, interest and expectations with respect to the programme on the part of politicians, partners, the media and the public. Lastly, the programme is being implemented through a novel system of decentralized regional/local strategies or partnerships, which have not been tried on this scale before in Wales. While other parts of the UK share one or more of these changes, Wales is unique (not just in the UK, but possibly across the EU as a whole) of having to accommodate so many institutional shifts and challenges at one time, especially in a programming period when the management requirements (financial management and control, monitoring, evaluation etc.) are much more demanding than previously.

To take just one of the above issues – the shift from Objective 2/5b to Objective 1 status – the experience of other UK regions making this transition is salutary. In the mid–1990s, the implementation arrangements for the new Merseyside Objective 1 programme (formerly Objective 2) were criticized as being too secretive, bureaucratic and centralized, and overseen by an 'inadequate secretariat' (Boland, 1996). In the same year, the new management arrangements for the Highlands and Islands Objective 1 programme (formerly Objective 5b) were similarly considered to be overly complex, opaque, bureaucratic, dominated by established economic development interests and the politics of the 'pork barrel' in the allocation of the resources (Bryden 1997). In both regions, these problems persisted for much of the past programming period, but it appears from recent evaluation studies and some academic research that appropriate lessons have been learned and applied in the current programme (Evans, 2002). While problems have not been totally overcome – bureaucracy is endemic to Structural Fund implementation, especially in Objective 1 areas – but both programmes have largely 'settled down'. The disadvantage for Wales is that the learning time is short, since there may not be a post-2006 Structural Funds programme on a significant scale in which lessons can be applied, although the experience with EU regional policy could certainly be applied to future implementation arrangements for domestic policy, in particular the use of delegated partnership arrangements for delivery.

In conclusion, looking at the Welsh Objective 1 programme from the outside, it seems that the political and administrative establishment may have been over-ambitious in trying to change virtually everything – programme area, programme resources, programme management and programme delivery – at the same time as needing to adapt to devolution and a more difficult EU regulatory environment. Nevertheless, it is important to keep the challenges in perspective, and indeed to recognize the achievement of getting a new programme launched and delivered in these circumstances. The current difficulties and controversies are not new – other UK regions have experienced many of the same problems – and, given sufficient openness on the part of programme managers and a willingness to recognize difficulties frankly and to respond to partner concerns, there is no reason why they should not be overcome. The mid-term review provides an important opportunity for systematically re-examining how the programme is working, in all its aspects, and providing a basis for dialogue with partners on instituting changes for the remainder of the programming period.

REFERENCES

Boland, P. (1996). 'Regional economic development and institutional mechanisms in Merseyside: Objective 1 status', in Alden, J. and Boland, P. (eds), *Regional Development Strategies: A European Perspective*, London, Regional Studies Association, Jessica Kingsley Publishers, 107–28.

Bryden, J. (1997). 'The implementation of Objective 1 in the Highlands and Islands of Scotland', in Bachtler, J. and Turok, I. (eds.), *The Coherence of EU Regional Policy: Contrasting Perspectives on the Structural Funds*, London, Regional Studies Association, Jessica Kingsley Publishers, 143–59.

CEC (2001). *Twelfth Annual Report on the Structural Funds*, Report from the European Commission, COM/2001/0539 final, Brussels, Commission of the European Communities.

CEC (1999). *The Structural Funds and their Coordination with the Cohesion Fund: Guidelines for programmes in the period 2000–2006*, Communication from the European Commission, 1 July 1999, Brussels, Commission of the European Communities.
(*http://europa.eu.int/comm/regional_policy/sources/docoffic/*)

Evans, R. (2002). 'The Merseyside Objective One programme: exemplar of coherent city-regional planning and governance or cautionary tale?', *European Planning Studies*, 10 (4), 595–617.

4. OBJECTIVE 1: THE STORY SO FAR

John Clarke

The Welsh European Funding Office (WEFO) is an Executive Agency of the Welsh Assembly Government, established in April 2000. Its role, as Managing Authority, is to ensure that Wales derives the maximum possible benefit from the European Structural Funds. In that same year, Wales saw the launch of the largest and most significant Structural Fund programme – Objective 1. West Wales and the Valleys qualifies for Objective 1 funding from the European Commission because its GDP per head is less than 75 per cent of the EU average.

The European Objective 1 Structural Funds will make a vital contribution to ensuring long-term growth in West Wales and the Valleys. The aim is to promote growth in employment and increase economic activity through a series of priorities and measures, such as developing small and medium-sized businesses, community economic regeneration and rural development. A total of £1,144m has been made available over seven years (2000–6). This will be matched by £861m of public sector funds and £428.5m of private sector funds leading to total investment of nearly £2.5 billion.

Objective 1 provides an opportunity to transform Wales into a growing and dynamic economic region, from Pontypool to Holyhead to Milford Haven. It represents an important challenge to the economy of Wales and it is essential that our plans hit the mark and deliver the maximum possible results to turn around our economy, upgrade our skill base and ensure that Wales has the competitive edge in the race for future economic success. Getting it right now will pay dividends for decades to come.

The challenging targets set out in the Objective 1 Single Programming Document (SPD) were a result of long discussions between the partners, the Welsh Assembly Government and the European Commission, and the key ones are:

- to raise GDP per head from 73 per cent of the UK average to 78 per cent;
- to support the creation of a skilled and adaptable workforce;
- to create 43,500 jobs and increase economic activity;
- to promote equality of opportunity and access, environmental sustainability and the Information Society.

These cannot be achieved by the Welsh Assembly Government alone. Objective 1 is very much a partnership effort. All that has been achieved in the past two years has been the result of hard work by many individuals and organizations across West Wales and the Valleys, in all sectors of the economy. Working in partnership means ensuring that different bodies, programmes and initiatives work together to achieve shared goals. These aims are closely connected to the Welsh Assembly Government's economic development strategy, *A Winning Wales* (NAW, 2002), and with many of the public, private and voluntary bodies in Wales. Local and regional partnerships have been created to ensure that there is a strategic approach at geographic and thematic level, and to ensure that each and every project submitted has the full support of the whole partnership and that ownership rests with the partners. These partnerships are shown below in Table 4.1.

TABLE **4.1**
Partnerships

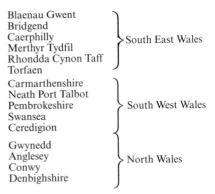

Regional partnerships	Local partnerships	
Agri - Food	Blaenau Gwent	
Information Age	Bridgend	
Entrepreneurship	Caerphilly	South East Wales
Innovation R&D	Merthyr Tydfil	
Business Support	Rhondda Cynon Taff	
Infrastructure	Torfaen	
Tourism	Carmarthenshire	
Community Regeneration	Neath Port Talbot	
Human Resource Development	Pembrokeshire	South West Wales
Forestry, Countryside and Coastal	Swansea	
Management	Ceredigion	
	Gwynedd	
	Anglesey	North Wales
	Conwy	
	Denbighshire	

A further approach that the Welsh Assembly Government has been encouraging is for local partnerships in each of the sub-regions to work together. The advantages of such an approach include the pooling of administrative resources for the development of projects and the dissemination of best practice as well as strategy co-ordination. It is important to try to ensure that projects supported by Objective 1 will make a real difference to economic development and that partnerships have not rushed in with pet projects, but have taken a sensible time to consider the needs of the region. It is important to strike the balance between early commitment and effective strategies.

Objective 1 is on course to deliver real benefits to people and businesses in Wales. In eighteen months, over 530 projects have been approved with EU grants in excess of £320m.[1] This means that investment of over £727m has already been secured for Wales. Those projects approved are now creating jobs, building up skills and strengthening communities right across the West Wales and the Valleys area.

It is fully recognized that the private sector plays a crucial role in creating wealth and economic success. Wales has made a conscientious effort to involve the private sector and to make sure they understand how the programme works. The Commission have been impressed by how systematically this has been addressed. The private sector wants to be involved, and has improved the performance of the programme. Recognizing the vital role of the private sector in this process, the Welsh European Funding Office (WEFO) has recruited a specialist team to its Private Sector Unit. This team is dedicated to advising and helping the private sector to make effective use of the opportunities presented by Structural Funds.

Objective 1 funds are also being targeted at the heart of our communities to empower people with the confidence and skills they need in order to contribute to the Welsh economy. The Voluntary Sector Support Unit has been set up and is managed by the Wales Council for Voluntary Action (WCVA). Its aim is to provide advice and information to the voluntary sector on the Objective 1 programme in order to help it access funds.

Some exciting new schemes are already under way and benefiting from Objective 1 funding. These include Finance Wales, which has been set up by the Welsh Development Agency and the Welsh Assembly Government to help small firms secure investment. The Knowledge Exploitation Fund run by ELWa will facilitate the culture and support the development of entrepreneurship in higher and further education. A good example of direct private sector involvement is a recent £3m approval for a Media Technium project, which is being led by Gelli Aur Limited. The aim of this project is to convert the Gelli Aur mansion house near Llandeilo into a regional media centre thus forming a basis for the growing media industry in Wales.

With regards to commitment and spend, Wales is performing well in comparison with our English counterparts. Table 4.2 below reflects this:

TABLE **4.2**
Objective 1 Commitment and Spent

Region	Committed		Spent	
	£m	**% of total**	**£m**	**% of total**
Cornwall	60	19.53	5.98	1.95
Merseyside	164.73	20.14	30.68	3.75
South Yorkshire	92.5	12.86	13.046	1.81
West Wales & Valleys	260	24	30.4	2.7

Source: House of Commons Official Report, 14 November 2001.

Objective 1 is a marathon, not a sprint. There are more than seven years to spend this vital injection of European cash. It is important that it is spent wisely.

NOTE

1. Figures as at 22 May 2002.

REFERENCES

National Assembly for Wales (NAW) (2001). *A Winning Wales: The National Economic Development Strategy of the Welsh Assembly Government*, Cardiff, NAW.
http://www.wales.gov.uk/themesbudgetandstrategic/content/neds/index.html

5. A VOLUNTARY SECTOR PERSPECTIVE ON EUROPEAN PROGRAMMES 2000–2006

Graham Benfield

I welcome the opportunity to provide the voluntary perspective of Objective 1. Through our Voluntary Sector Support Unit, the Wales Council for Voluntary Action (WCVA) has been in consultation with a wide range of local organizations involved in the Objective 1 process. The points I raise here are taken from this process and the issues and concerns raised by those organizations with which we have recently consulted.

The WCVA was a member of the European Task Force, established to take forward proposals for the 2000–6 programmes. WCVA then led the Community Capacity Building study prepared for the European Task Force, involving a very wide range of organizations and sectors. At that time there was a consistent and unambiguous message from the sector about the need to improve the accessibility of the programmes to smaller organizations and in particular to organizations representing and working with excluded people and communities. All the organizations we consulted with agreed that they wanted:

- Effective community participation in the delivery of Objective 1;
- Access to comprehensive advice and assistance so that they can participate, draw up and implement their proposals;
- High-quality consultation processes to ensure that the widest possible range of groups are able to participate in the programme;
- The process made easier, in particular a simplification of the application procedure;
- Dedicated funding routes to maximize the availability and accessibility of domestic funds for match funding to support local projects that meet locally-identified needs;

*   Technical assistance to support organizations' involvement in the pro-
    gramme.

On the surface it would appear that the voluntary sector has been successful
in achieving a lot of these things, for example:

*   Voluntary and community organizations now have equal membership
    of the Objective 1 Programme Monitoring Committee, and at local and
    regional levels – although this does not tell the full story, a point to
    which I will return later;
*   Grant schemes for small organizations: the Social Risk Fund has been
    developed and has helped nearly seventy organizations in its first year,
    also some local partnerships have established key funds for the sector;
*   Advance payments for voluntary organizations applying for European
    Regional Development Fund (ERDF) funding in line with European
    Structural Fund (ESF) funding arrangements have been agreed;
*   A Voluntary Sector Support Unit has been established and is now in the
    process of helping organizations prepare applications.

However, Objective 1 is still 'not happening' for the voluntary sector in
terms of easy access and sustainable funding sources. We have a number of
major problems to face and overcome. Only 50 projects under Objective 1
Priority 3 (Community Economic Regeneration) have been approved. There is
a low level of commitment across the board. Projects approved or under consideration account for only 27 per cent of the indicative allocation to the
regional partnership, while, in aggregate, only 32 per cent of the indicative
allocations to the local partnerships are either already committed or would be
needed to fund projects under consideration. A relatively high number of
projects submitted through the partnerships for the initial September 2000
bidding round were withdrawn as a number of partnerships believed they were
liable to exceed their indicative allocations; despite this, and the emerging
pattern of 'underspend', relatively few of these projects have been resubmitted.

WHY IS OBJECTIVE 1 'NOT HAPPENING' FOR VOLUNTARY AND COMMUNITY ORGANIZATIONS?

Let us start by looking at the two fundamental issues that organizations continually raise with us: The application process and the partnerships
themselves.

The application process
Firstly, let us consider the application process and what an applicant would have to go through to submit an application. The first thing to do if you want to be successful is find out about the programme and look through the guidance notes and papers provided. This requires reading in excess of 1,000 pages before attempting to fill out a pro-forma application. For an Objective 1 application, this consists of:

- Single Programming Document (250 pages);
- Programme Complement (190 pages);
- Single Programming Document Annexes (250 pages);
- cross-cutting themes; equal opportunities (20 pages); environment (150 pages); information and communication technology (110 pages);
- a Local Action Plan (approx 30 pages);
- Better Wales (60 pages);
- National Economic Development Strategy (40 pages).

If you are submitting a regional application you can add to this another fourteen local action plans (250 pages) and a regional action plan (30 pages).

Faced with having to read all this material, it is hardly surprising that only people who are immersed in the process fully understand it. In fact, it is a surprise that we have had as many as fifty applications in a priority that is dedicated to developing the most deprived communities. If you were a small community organization would you really think that after reading all this material Objective 1 is the fund for you? Of course, there are a whole range of support services and information sources available. But, where do you go for help? Your first port of call is likely to be the local or regional partnership to which you are going to submit the application, the Welsh European Funding Office (WEFO) or the Voluntary Sector Support Unit at WCVA. Unfortunately, the quality of information varies depending on which source you choose. Within the Voluntary Sector Support Unit, we are continually dealing with organizations which have been given the wrong information whilst preparing an application. An example of this is an applicant being told that they needed a full-blown business plan for an £50,000 ESF project when quite clearly they did not.

If an applicant does manage to interpret the information and still feels that they have a relevant project that could be funded under Objective 1, there are still a number of hurdles. Firstly, the applicant needs to consult with the relevant partnership(s) to ensure that there is no duplication and to make sure they have match funding for the project. Each partnership adopts a different approach to processing and assessing applications: in short, there is no real consistency. How are we to develop innovative projects if we do not take a consistent approach to the development and consultation phase of the application process? Some partnerships will only assess the pro forma itself and will not consult on the project until a pro forma is submitted. Others are more helpful and are fully supportive in the development stage (pre-pro forma). Equally, some partnerships will only look at applications that have the match funding in place, which is totally contradictory to the National Assembly's line that 'good projects should not fail because of a lack of match funding'.

This is another major problem for the sector. The Assembly has said that match funding will be made available for successful projects and WEFO now have someone in place to co-ordinate this process. Yet when we ask the Assembly or WEFO for a simple guide to what National Assembly budgets are available no one can help. When the question is pushed, it appears the system is that someone in WEFO merely goes from department to department in the Assembly until they find a budget with which the project fits and which has money available to fund it. That this is not very satis-factory and is also very difficult and time-consuming for the applicant. To highlight this issue we can consider one specific potential source of match funding – the Local Regeneration Fund. The voluntary sector has a separate pot of money for which it can bid, but applications for this had to be submitted by the end of April 2002. Yet Objective 1 is a rolling programme. What happens to the good projects that come through at the end of the year when there is no money available because it has all been allocated in April? Even more concretely, a good example of problems caused by match funding can be shown by a recent childcare project. This project was sub-mitted to the Human Resource Development (HRD) partnership and approved by WEFO and the strategic partnership. It is now struggling to get started because it is lacking in match funding. Currently, it is being pushed from agency to department to WEFO because no one will say that they will provide the match funding.

It is also sometimes difficult to determine who is the most appropriate person to approach. We have had a number of complaints from applicants that their pro forma has not even reached the full partnership for discussion. We have noted some actual examples where this is because the person doing the appraisal at local partnership level is failing the application either because they do not understand it, or because it conflicts with what a public body is doing. At a regional level, problems are further intensified because of the requirement to consult with all the relevant partnerships (that is, up to fifteen different partnerships) prior to submission. It is a system that creates friction and suspicion between local and regional partnerships and it is detrimental to project development.

Having got through the pro-forma and consultation process, organizations then have to prepare a full application which is over thirty pages long for appraisal by WEFO – which will then raise many other issues. Some organizations have had three and four page letters asking a range of questions, some of which are not that relevant to the application. Once WEFO are satisfied, it then makes recommendations to the strategy partnership for the final approval.

From start to finish, this process has taken anything up to nine months – and even longer in some cases. Is it any wonder that there is a low take-up from the voluntary sector? The current systems and processes seem more suited to public bodies and agencies who have the time and resources to go through this process. Can we really expect voluntary and community organizations, that truly understand the needs and problems of communities, to take part fully in this programme? The answer is an unequivocal NO, and if we do not start looking at these issues and dealing with them we will continue to deliver the same old tired projects that we did under previous programmes.

The partnerships

Objective 1 partnerships are the cornerstone of this process and based on the 'three thirds principle'. They are quite clearly the way forward, not just for Objective 1 but also for other initiatives and schemes in Wales. We must continue with them if we are really to change things in Wales. But these partnerships must be true partnerships where everyone has an equal say and is able to make a valid contribution. It must be remembered that equal membership does not mean an equal partnership. The members of these partnerships need time to learn and understand each other before they become effective. How can we do this when at least two-thirds of the membership still depends on people giving up their own time, or organizations using already overstretched staff, to attend meetings? They cannot even claim any travel expenditure or for the time they give up to be involved in the process, or even use the money given as match funding to allow for additional resources to provide wider support. Instead, would-be applicants have to rely heavily on the lead body for support as lead bodies are the only ones with access to technical assistance. As a result, this often places the lead bodies themselves in an untenable position because of the tension between the role they have as secretariat and the needs of their own organizations.

If we are to make Objective 1 work for community and voluntary groups then we need to make the processes clearer and simpler for everybody. We need:

- to develop a clear protocol for working that distinguishes between the roles of the membership and the role of the secretariat;
- to look at technical assistance and how a wide range of organizations, not just the lead bodies, can access it;
- to develop projects and schemes that make the process of access clearer and stimulates demand from community organizations through activities like pre-matched key funds;
- to look at what works and what does not – in particular noting that many of these initiatives need to be developed and delivered by the organizations that fully understand the needs of voluntary and community groups.

I hasten to add that this is not as easy an option as some may think. For example, when considering the use of pre-matched key funds, WCVA's experience with the social risk fund has shown that the development and lead-in time can be more than three months even for the smallest of projects, with such a scheme needing a great deal of resourcing.

For those groups with sufficient resources to apply for mainstream funding, we need to provide clear guidance on match funding and its availability. If we can do this, then the second half of this programme will be a success and, perhaps more importantly, leave us with a legacy of true partnership working that really starts to shape new ways of doing things. The alternative I am afraid is failure – something that we must not even consider.

6. A LOCAL AUTHORITY PERSPECTIVE ON OBJECTIVE 1

Chris Burns

Although the achievement of Objective 1 status for West Wales and the Valleys from January 2000 undoubtedly marked a significant watershed in terms of regional policy in Wales, European Union support for economic and social regeneration is far from being a new phenomenon. There are literally hundreds, if not thousands, of factory buildings, business parks, access roads and many other testaments to European Community (EC) funding dating back to the late 1970s and early 1980s to be found across much of Wales, and especially across the South Wales Valleys. Many thousands of people have taken part in training programmes and courses funded by the European Social Fund over that period, and thousands of businesses have received financial support for projects backed by EC programmes.

However, Objective 1 was heralded as being different. It was to be different in the scale of the total funding available, which was greater than ever before. But, more importantly, it was to be different in the way that it would be administered and delivered. This became evident during the build up to Objective 1 status during 1998 and 1999. Several local authorities took part in lobbies of the European Parliament in Brussels during that time and, on one occasion, one of the senior officials at the Commission, Graham Meadows, outlined in some detail what the Commission hoped might emerge as a different mode of operation.

He stressed three key things that we should consider in preparing the programme for Objective 1 for Wales. One of the most important things was that the scheme had to be about economic regeneration and productivity – creating wealth and economic activity. He also stressed that there was a great need to concentrate the support on those areas that needed help the most. Finally, there had to be more of a 'grass-roots' community-based involvement than had previously been the case. As he put it (and I hope he will not mind being quoted), it had taken local authorities many years of hard work to get in through the door with the former Welsh Office in terms of running EC programmes; we should be careful not to now close the door behind us and keep the community outside, as they too wanted a part to play.

Certainly, so far as my own local authority, Caerphilly County Borough Council, was concerned we took those words very much to heart and started to put together a new approach as soon as we returned from those discussions in Brussels. One of the main features of the new approach was that we drew together a strong partnership group with three or four business people from the local Business Forum, key players from the voluntary sector and partners from major agencies such as the Welsh Development Agency – the Caerphilly Objective 1 Partnership being officially formed in the summer of 1999. The intention was to put together a strong and broadly based team which could prepare an exciting package of projects and strategy for the use of Objective 1 funding in the area.

Besides ensuring more broadly based community involvement than had ever been the case previously, the main aim of this Partnership was to move away from the old method of European funding on a project-by-project basis and towards, instead, the development of a coherent strategy based on a package of complementary and interrelated projects.

For twenty years, there had been a 'free-for-all' competition amongst project sponsors, many of whom would submit similar (or even identical) ideas for funding, there being no overall control as to whether these competing bids complemented each other or helped to make up a sensible patchwork of mutually supportive projects. Sponsors would tout their ideas around until they found someone willing to write a letter of support proving that their project contributed to some strategy or another. Instead of this, there was now to be a new approach based on proper strategies and packages of projects – with the needs of the local community taking precedence over the desire of individual sponsors to obtain funding. Robust and integrated packages of ideas would be formulated, with a strong input from the local communities, and these strategies would be funded on a more holistic basis than the former pepper-potting of individual projects.

Sadly, the experience of the Caerphilly Objective 1 Partnership in the first few years at least was to be far removed from this 'brave new world'. Though the Caerphilly Partnership prepared an overall strategy, with all of the potential sponsors working together and agreeing that for each idea or project only one of them would make a bid, there emerged a funding mechanism which had no place for such local strategies at all. Instead, individual bids were called forward which could be picked out in isolation from complementary ideas in the local strategy – with a return to the free-for-all which favoured those who could best fill in the application forms and traverse the maze of the application process (which, needless to say, became even more complicated than ever before, more resembling a Franz Kafka novel than a country intent on economic regeneration and renewal). The only real response to the Caerphilly local strategy when it was submitted was a request that it be cut down to no more than twenty pages.

As disappointing as the lack of any real intent to develop local strategies of interrelated projects which could fit together and complement each other was the almost complete lack of delegation of decisions to the local level. It was remarked upon by one person that, at the time this debate was going on during 2000, the government seemed quite happy to delegate £50 million tranches of funding to the directors of the Millennium Dome, one after the other, but no one was prepared to delegate even small sums of money to representative partnerships of local business and community leaders in the South Wales Valleys. As a result all funding decisions were held up for months, or even a year, and were taken at a level which could not have as good a grasp of the needs and priorities of the local area as could the local Partnership.

More recently, some delegation of funding (for Priority 3, for example) has taken place with relatively small sums of money being earmarked to be allocated (provided eligibility conditions are met) by the local Partnership. This sort of approach across the full range of the programme, with desk officers from Welsh European Funding Office (WEFO) being seconded to local partnerships to carry out eligibility checks at an earlier stage and with global funds pre-allocated for determination by the partnerships, could have resulted in a much faster and more effective start to the Objective 1 programme and a far more joined-up approach to the funding of strategic packages of projects.

Another major difficulty with the Objective 1 programme has been the complete disregard for the dire and pressing need to invest in some aspects of the infrastructure of the Valleys especially, and for the low priority given to the tourist industry. The lack of funding for infrastructure within the Programming Document was pointed out at each level of the drafting stage but was, it seems, largely due to the refusal of the Commission to entertain any significant spend on such projects. This is very much in contrast with the

Irish programme where much of the emphasis is on building infrastructure (be it in road, rail or telecommunications links) between the growth areas (especially around Dublin) and the West. It has been said that this is a reflection of the fact that the Commission does not consider West Wales and the Valleys to be a 'real' Objective 1 area, but more of a highly deprived Objective 2 area, in need of economic restructuring.

Some parts of the Valleys are highly dependent on jobs in the coastal belt in Cardiff and Newport. Caerphilly County Borough, for example, has daily out-commuting levels of over 40 per cent of the workforce. Without efficient transportation links enabling people to travel to work easily and quickly, this leads to major problems, and fuels the decision by many to decide to move away and live closer to their place of work – further reinforcing the depopulation of some Valleys communities, with the younger people and those having the highest skills and rates of pay being the most likely to leave. Moreover, inward investment decisions are still heavily affected by the efficiency of road networks and especially links to the M4 in South Wales. The inability of the Objective 1 programme to help address these problems is a major weakness.

The lack of recognition of the role of small town centres (as centres of employment, as providers of services and facilities to local communities and as a key part of the morale and confidence of local communities) is another major weakness in the programme. During the early 1990s, the Cynon Valley, for example, was able to receive considerable EC support for town-centre regeneration schemes, environmental projects, car parks to attract shoppers, road improvements and building renovations. Few if any of these would now receive Objective 1 funding – and in this sense Objective 1 has actually been a major step backwards in comparison with previous funding programmes.

So, is it all bad news and what can be done to address the problems which have been identified? In concentrating on those aspects which need to be improved, there is a danger of seeing only negatives. The decision to redraw the map of assisted areas to create a zone (known as West Wales and the Valleys) which was eligible to qualify for Objective 1 was one which speaks highly of the willingness and desire of the Welsh, UK and EU administrations to work together to tackle the problems. And the gradual drift in the direction of local delegation for some parts of the programme is one which is to be applauded. There have also been signs, at long last, of integration and convergence with other mainstream programmes. The delegation of Local Regeneration Fund (LRF) match-funding support to local partnerships so that the two funding streams could be handled more closely together is a very welcome development.

In terms of what can be done from here on, the approaching mid-term review should be seized upon as an opportunity to make funding available for infrastructure, urban regeneration and tourism projects to a greater extent than for the first three years of the programme. The application procedures are still unacceptably drawn out and complex, especially if a broader range of applicants from local communities is to be attracted. Most of all, greater trust must be placed in local communities to make sensible decisions as to what can be most effective in regenerating their areas. If the Caerphilly Objective 1 partnership is anything to go by, these partnerships are not hotbeds of revolutionaries who will spend the money on outlandish and esoteric projects, but are fairly sober groups of people with years of experience in business and community or voluntary activity who are well placed to know what will and will not work for their community.

The experience of Objective 1 has said a lot about Wales. I was fortunate to visit Ireland with some colleagues from our partners in the Employment Service early in 2000 to see what their Irish equivalents in the national training agency Foras Áiseanna Saothair (FÁS) had managed to accomplish with Objective 1 funds. At the time of the visit neither Wales or Ireland had received approval of their programme documents, but in Ireland there was no sense of delay or any of the confusion which reigned in Wales. When we asked how they had managed to start training programmes without the programme being in place, we were told confidently: 'Don't worry, there is sure to be retrospection to fund projects which started in advance of the approval.' You certainly could not have found anyone in Wales willing to even confirm that there would be retrospection at that time, let alone to which projects it might apply.

As I heard the Irish Consul in Wales, Conor O'Riordhan, say at a conference on Objective 1 in 1999, commenting on the ability of those of us in Wales to tie ourselves in knots: 'In Ireland we are different to the Welsh; when we come to a fork in the road, we take it.' Perhaps we could benefit from some of that sort of confidence in Wales.

7. TIME FOR REALISM

Michael German

Professor Walter Halstein, the first president of the European Commission, once said: 'Those who do not believe in miracles in European Affairs are not realists.' The Welsh version of that phrase might read: 'Those who do not believe in bad news on Objective 1 affairs are not realists.'

I look forward to the miraculous day when we can acknowledge and celebrate just how much has been achieved on Objective 1 related issues over the past few years. It is essential that all of us involved in the Objective 1 programme, from whatever standpoint, remember that it is the outcomes which really count with Objective 1 and not the processes by which we achieve them.

In looking back at the story so far, let us look at three headline outcomes. The first, dramatic outcome, was the Objective 1 status designation of West Wales and the Valleys. The fact that we have the biggest EU Structural Fund Programme in the UK is at last an acknowledgement of our position at the bottom of the UK regional economic league and an opportunity that we must not allow to be undermined or wasted. Second, through the scrutiny of the National Assembly, political pressure ensured that we had a £421 'Barnett busting' settlement at the last Comprehensive Spending Review (CSR). This ensured that the benefits of Objective 1 were not at the expense of other public services; many in the regional development field had feared that Objective 1 status in that sense would be a curate's egg. In England, there are ongoing match-funding problems which have held back programme development. In Wales, we had the European money transferred to us 'cleanly'; there was a new transparency to funding, albeit some blood was spilt in the process. We should not underestimate the significance of the last CSR settlement; its political impact was immense, and it established a precedent which goes beyond European funding and raises very real questions as to the very sustainability of the Barnett formula. Third, here we are, eighteen months into the programme, and we have over 500 projects approved and over £300m of committed expenditure. To quote the album title of the late Ian Drury and his Blockheads, we have at last 'Reasons to be Cheerful'!

Of course, getting here was not easy. There are still imperfections in the implementation system and we should never allow cheerfulness to become complacency. With the benefit of hindsight, I think it important and constructive to examine some of the main problems that have occurred. These are my personal views on the story so far.

OBJECTIVE 1 CONFUSION

A confusion about what the 'glittering prize'/loadsamoney hype of Objective 1 status actually means for business goes right back to the late 1990s when we first won Objective 1 status. With hindsight, I think we share a collective guilt which still wrecks Objective 1 perceptions.

Quite frankly, I think too many people made the fundamental mistake of explaining too much about Objective 1 and all the associated acronyms and terminology of the Structural Funds' rules and regulations. This could and should have been avoided. The concentration of minds should have been on the dialogue and analysis necessary to determine what support communities, businesses and individuals actually needed from Objective 1, or, for that matter, any source of public sector intervention.

There were too many high expectations drowned by brain-numbing explanations of the intricacies of the ERDF,[1] ESF[2] and EAGGF,[3] SPDs[4] or CSFs,[5] programme complements, single beneficiary rules, accountable body status, N+2 and all the rest of it, the length and breadth of Wales. This created too many 'Objective 1 weary' representatives of the public, private and voluntary sectors. The development of strategy amongst sectors should have focused exclusively on what interventions we needed in order to advance social and economic regeneration in Wales in the first place.

TOO MUCH PARTNERSHIP – NOT ENOUGH STRATEGY?

In October 2000, I formed an Objective 1 Task and Finish Group, made up of individuals from academia, business, voluntary bodies and the public sector, to work through holistically how the Objective 1 process needed to be improved. I think that initiative worked and genuinely helped correct many of the early malfunctions and 'turf battles' that were starting to emerge in the initial implementation processes. The fact that we have now had over £300m of project approvals since then provides evidence to support my view. But we should never be complacent; there was a specific commitment in the Task and Finish Report for a review of the recommendations one year on from implementation. I personally would not be averse to that review's being conducted; there would be something healthy in taking an empirical review of the new system, in order to determine which parts of the group's recommendations could work better in practice.

Before the group was formed, there was much debate within and between the nascent local and regional partnerships in Wales as to who would lead implementation of the programme. The Task and Finish Group looked at this issue. There was a perception that the group's recommendations created more committees – it did not. The Task and Finish Group recommended fewer regional partnerships and, very usefully, recognized the difference between project development and project approval. There are now only four strategic partnerships involved with project approval, as recommended by the Task and Finish Group – these four strategic partnerships have taken members from both local and regional partnerships that were previously competing for control. The feedback I have had so far is that they work, and work well.

The early approach by partners across Wales was to cut the available money into slices, with no strategic approach – either local to regional or regional to local. The actors on this stage have now come together and are reaching common agreements on the way to tackle Wales's common problems. The jigsaw is being completed and the pieces are not just lying around unconnected. Local and regional partnerships were important for project development, particularly at the beginning of the process. You can never have too much partnership. But if partners feel that, since the Task and Finish Group recommendations, the number of local and regional partnerships should be reviewed, should this not be an issue for those partnerships?

The Task and Finish Group also ensured a much greater emphasis on strategy and delivery issues which have been addressed, and which need to be pursued further. What about continued complaints from private and voluntary sector groups about application procedures?

This relates back to my initial comments on the initial mistakes made in raising awareness about the potential benefits of Objective 1 status. From the very beginning, we needed to distinguish much more clearly between the 'applicant' and the 'beneficiary'. The intermediary is the 'turn-key partner', but not the final beneficiary. Some news coverage has criticized the fact that too many applications were awarded to public sector 'beneficiaries'. Under such terminology and classification, Finance Wales, Wales's first 'development bank' would qualify as a beneficiary of the structural funds, but Finance Wales was not applying for its own benefit but for the benefit of its clients (that is, businesses) in the West Wales and the Valleys programme area.

Given European Union rules precluding 'single beneficiaries' for Structural Funds, support must be delivered through intermediaries, be they Finance Wales, the WDA, local authorities, the voluntary sector or public/private partnerships. EU state aid regulations provide another need and rationale for public sector advice and support. Individual businesses and voluntary organizations should not be made to apply through the complex and demanding processes of the Objective 1 system; we need to provide more 'key funds', money which is pre-matched, easy to apply for and easily administered, targeted to and tailored for the private and voluntary sectors.

Initiatives such as the creation of Finance Wales, the reform of Business Connect, the creation of Farming Connect, the Wales Council for Voluntary Action social risk fund and work currently being conducted on support for the social economy must work to assist and improve the flow of funds to final beneficiaries. This will beg a new question: when the funds pass through an intermediary, – is there enough awareness that the final beneficiary has received Objective 1?

I believe passionately that for further improvements for the future, routes such as these should be the appropriate channels for simplifying the flow of funds. Voluntary and private sector projects need simple and accurate advice and support from whatever relevant source. What they do not need is a European Regional Development Fund or European Structural Fund form for dealing with the process of applications through the partnerships. Partnership does not mean that all three sectors submit each Objective 1 bid or application, but that sectors contribute their own innate strengths and specific capabilities. The public sector in particular should act as the turn-key partner, facilitating the flow of funds at local or regional level and cushioning the individual private or voluntary sector applicant from unnecessary bureaucracy.

The capacity-building social partners unit is now up and running, a private company run by Business Wales and the Wales TUC, in order to give a fresh start to business–government relationships in Wales. I very much hope that this is an area of work to which they can bring greater understanding and activity.

CONCLUSION

Clearly, this year will be a critical one for the future of the programme. We have the Comprehensive Spending Review in July and the first N+2 threshold date in December. But I think the most miraculous aspect of Objective 1 is the way in which it has raised awareness of structural-fund issues across Wales and permeated the public consciousness. I have colleagues who have been cross-examined in the butcher's shop on whether or not the last CSR would give us the match funding we needed. Objective 1 is used as a term in common parlance in a way that eluded Objective 2 in Industrial South Wales or Objective 5b in Rural Wales. Expectations remain high, and all components of every partnership in Wales have a duty to pull together to ensure that one more miracle in European affairs does become a reality.

NOTES

1. ERDF: European Regional Development Fund.
2. ESF: European Structural Funds.
3. EAGGF: European Agricultural Guidance and Guarantee Fund.
4. SPD: Single Programming Document.
5. CSR: Comprehensive Spending Review.

8. EUROPEAN STRUCTURAL FUNDS: ARE THEY WORKING IN WALES?

Phil Williams

INTRODUCTION

In assessing the effect of the various European structural funds in Wales we should ask five questions:

- Do structural funds work?
- Are we on target in implementing the various programmes?
- Is there enough money in the Assembly budget to support the programmes?
- How are the funds being distributed?
- How will we know if they are working?

DO STRUCTURAL FUNDS WORK?

This is one of the key questions that the European Union asks in the *Second Report on Economic and Social Cohesion* (European Union, 2001). In comparing the average GDP per head of the Member States over the past ten years there is undoubtedly strong convergence. The gap in GDP per head between Spain, Portugal and Greece and the rest of the EU has been significantly reduced while the Irish economy has been transformed from one of the poorest to one of the most productive. However, it does not follow that this convergence between the Member States has resulted from the allocation of Structural Funds. The opportunities of a Single Market for a low-wage economy and the effect of the Common Agricultural Policy (CAP) on Member States with a large agricultural sector, not the Structural Funds, may be the prime drivers towards economic cohesion. In cases like Portugal, Greece and Ireland where most – if not all – of the country receives Objective 1 support it is not easy to separate the effects of the Single Market and the CAP from the effects of Structural Funds.

However, a disturbing feature of the Cohesion Report is the evidence of increasing divergence in regional GDP per head. The EU now publishes an index of regional disparity in GDP per head, based on a weighted standard deviation between the GDP per head of the different NUTS 1 regions within a Member State. (Wales as a whole is a NUTS 1 region – a Territorial Unit for Statistics at the first level; West Wales and the Valleys is a NUTS 2 region; Bridgend and Neath Port Talbot together form a NUTS 3 region.) These figures show that over the past ten years the index of regional disparity has increased in eleven out of the fifteen Member States. The UK now has the highest disparity index (33.9 per cent) – far higher than Italy (27.6 per cent) or Germany (26.8 per cent) for example – and the greatest increase over the ten years.[1] It could be, of course, that without Structural Funds the regional disparities would be even greater. Nevertheless, in many countries, there is very little evidence that previous European programmes have significantly reduced the gap in GDP between regions within a Member State. This certainly applies to the 1994–9 programmes in Wales.

ARE WE ON TARGET IN WALES IN IMPLEMENTING THE VARIOUS PROGRAMMES?

In Wales there has been a slow start to all the European programmes in the 2000–6 round. In some cases, such as Objective 2 and some of the community initiatives, the problem has been Europe-wide but in the case of Objective 1 – far and away the largest of the programmes – the UK was well behind several other countries in getting approval for the Single Programming Document (SPD). This delay was compounded by a further delay in Wales in defining the relationship between regional and local partnerships, and a totally inexcusable delay in establishing a full set of regional partnerships (the last – the infrastructure partnership – was not fully in place until November 2001, despite strong and repeated warnings from Plaid Cymru over the previous twelve months).

As a result, there has been a serious delay in the total funds approved for projects during the first two years of the programme. Thus, according to the timetables agreed in the different SPDs for Objectives 1, 2 and 3, the Rural Development Plan (RDP) and the Community Initiatives, a total of £413m of European funds should have been 'committed' by the end of December 2001. In fact, by the end of March 2002, only £330m had been committed –

a shortfall of £83m even if we ignore the three-month gap between the calendar year and the UK financial year.

In Objective 1 the main shortfall has – not surprisingly – been in approving projects covered by the Regional Infrastructure Partnership, including support for information technology (IT) infrastructure, clean energy and integrated passenger transport. There has also been a shortfall in supporting community regeneration and rural development. It is likely that by December 2002 much of this shortfall will be closed by a number of major infrastructure projects. The problems in community regeneration and rural development may be more difficult to resolve.

However, commitment is only the first target to meet: experience shows that commitment does not guarantee expenditure. For example, over £70m of European grants 'committed' to Wales in the 1994–9 programme were still unclaimed in March 2002 and it is likely that most of this money will be 'decommitted', that is, returned to Brussels.

Since 2000, the rules on 'decommitment' have been tightened and the 'N+2' rule is especially stringent. If a sum of money should be approved for projects in 2000 – according to the agreed timetable of commitment in the SPDs – then it must be spent, and the invoices cleared, by the end of 2002. Similarly, the 2001 allocation must be spent by the end of 2003 and so on.

The date at which the initial approval of projects is actually given can be delayed – as we see is already happening in Wales – but this does not affect the date by which the money must be spent. Any unspent balance at the end of each year is decommitted. If we add up all the European programmes (Objectives 1, 2 and 3, the RDP and the community initiatives) then, assuming 1 Euro = £0.62:

- by the end of December 2002 we must have spent £209m;
- by the end of December 2003 we must have spent £413m;
- by the end of December 2004 we must have spent £612m;
- by the end of December 2005 we must have spent £806m;
- by the end of December 2006 we must have spent £978m;
- by the end of December 2007 we must have spent £1,160m;
- by the end of December 2008 we must have spent £1,340m.

There is one factor that eases the threat of decommitment in the first few years. During the first two years of the programme, the Treasury is able to draw down 7 per cent of the total European contribution – in theory to allow advance payments to final beneficiaries, in practice to sit in a Bank of England account. This counts as expenditure, whether it is actually spent or not, and this applies until the very end of the programme in December 2008 when actual expenditure must be demonstrated or the money returned. As a result, we start with £94 million 'expenditure' without a single pound being actually spent.

It follows that, by December 2002, we need to show actual expenditure of only £115m (that is, £209m – £94m), 55 per cent of the accounted expenditure. Perhaps this explains the complacency shown at the very low levels of actual expenditure in 2000 and 2001. By December 2003, however, we will need to show actual expenditure of £319m, 77 per cent of the accounted expenditure. By December 2004, the noose begins to tighten and the total actual expenditure must increase to £518m, or 85 per cent of the accounted expenditure. And so on.

It is at the end of 2004 and 2005 that the question of decommitment – described by an EU official as the 'humiliation' of decommitment – may arise for the 2000–6 programme. In the meantime, it is almost certain that a substantial sum from the 1994–9 programme will be decommitted at the end of 2002.

IS THERE ENOUGH MONEY IN THE ASSEMBLY BUDGET TO SUPPORT THE PROGRAMMES?

Closely linked with the threat of decommitment is the question of the total Assembly budget necessary to support the programmes. To avoid decommitment it will be necessary for the actual expenditure on the programmes to increase substantially from 2003 onwards. This affects the National Assembly budget in two ways: First, the European component of total expenditure is paid entirely by the National Assembly for Wales via its agency, the Welsh European Funding Office or WEFO. The average paid out in European grants over the three financial years 2000–3 (including overhang from the 1994–9 programme and an estimate of likely expenditure during the rest of 2002–3) is £120m a year. To avoid decommitment over the next three financial years 2003–6 – covered by the 2002 Comprehensive Spending Review (CSR) – this must increase to £190m a year. The present CSR allows only £160m 'on top of Barnett' for 2003–4, so unless this is increased in the 2002 CSR there will be a shortfall of £30m.

Second, in addition to the European component of the different programmes the UK must provide about an equal amount of match funding, and about 80 per cent of this comes from the public sector. It is a widespread belief that the 2000 CSR allocated match funding to Wales. This was not the case, and not a pound was added to the Barnett block to cover public sector match funding. As a result, over the three financial years 2000–3 about £100m a year in match funding is being paid from the public sector in Wales. Just over half of this – £60m a year – corresponds to the previous levels of spending on match funding by local authorities and government agencies. This is often described as match funding 'in the system'. However, to meet the greatly increased level of expenditure after 2000, the National Assembly has allocated, on average, a further £40m a year to provide additional public sector match funding via such budget lines as Pathway to Prosperity and Local Regeneration Funds. None of this expenditure has been provided by the Treasury 'on top of Barnett' and so it has been taken out of other core budgets, such as health and education. If we are to avoid decommitment, this element of expenditure must also increase sharply in the three financial years 2003–6. The total public sector contribution will rise to £150m a year, and if the funding available 'in the system' remains at £60m a year the National Assembly will have to contribute £90m a year out of its core budget to meet the increased total.

To summarize: to avoid decommitment over the three financial years 2003–6, the National Assembly will need to provide a total of £290m a year (£190 million a year in European grants plus £100m a year to supplement the match funding 'in the system'). If we assume that £20m a year of European grants paid to the Treasury 'trickles down' into the block grant via Barnett, then to fund the European programmes without raiding the core budgets for health and education we will need to have £260m a year on top of Barnett in the coming CSR. This is £100m a year more than we were allocated for 2003–4 under the previous CSR.

HOW ARE THE FUNDS BEING DISTRIBUTED?

The next question to ask is how the allocated funds are distributed between the different priorities of the different SPDs, and between the different counties of Wales. Objective 2 was very late in starting, as were several of the community initiatives, so at this stage it is only possible to outline the way in which Objective 1 funds have been allocated. The Objective 1 budget is divided between seven Priorities, and we can examine the allocation according to Priority as a percentage of the scheduled commitment. These percentages are shown in Table 8.1.

Two Priorities are over-subscribed. Priority 1 provides support for Small and Medium-Sized Enterprises (SMEs), including financial support, and

TABLE **8.1**

Aims of Objective 1

Priority	Purpose	% of scheduled commitment allocated
1	Support for SMEs	1.15
2	Innovation	0.85
3	Community Regeneration	0.40
4	Lifelong Learning	1.09
5	Rural Development	0.62
6	Infrastructure	0.04

Note: Priority 7 provides technical assistance for all projects.

this has been the subject of large bids both by the WDA and by Local Partnerships. Priority 4 provides support for education and training, and here there have been substantial bids from ELWa, universities and further education colleges. The cynic might well say 'the usual suspects'.

Priority 2 for Innovation is under-subscribed. This is mainly because of delay in approving projects for IT infrastructure and clean energy pending the establishment of an Infrastructure Partnership. These delays occurred despite repeated warnings over a long period of time, made by Plaid Cymru via the Economic Development Committee and the Objective 1 Monitoring Committee. This delay also explains the 4 per cent level of commitment under priority 5 for Infrastructure.

Priority 3 for Community Regeneration poses a special challenge. It is obvious that deprived communities are, with some outstanding exceptions, less equipped to generate good proposals and to navigate them through the WEFO procedures. In some cases there will be a need for proactive capacity building. Equally disturbing is the problem of the most deprived communities's generating adequate match funding. This is just one example where adequate match funding is simply not 'in the system', and to remedy the shortfall in the approval rate will require a substantial increase in the National Assembly budget for Community Regeneration.

Finally, priority 5 for Rural Development includes a large number of measures and there seem to be several factors leading to the low level of approvals, including some uncertainties about the strict definition of rurality.[2]

In addition to the uneven distribution of approvals between the different Priorities of Objective 1 there is also evidence of a very uneven distribution between the allocation of Objective 1 funds to different Local Partnerships.

It is not easy to determine the total list of approved projects for each of the fifteen local partnerships as the database on the WEFO website is not complete. However, by combining those projects listed for each Local Partnership with those projects where the county council is the lead partner, those projects not part of a regional action plan where the local further education college is the lead partner, and those projects which are clearly local in scope, it is possible to get a clear indication of the overall pattern.

At the beginning of March 2002 it appeared that the most successful Local Partnership, in the part of the Objective 1 region with the highest GDP per head, had won approval for grants totalling £77 per head. In contrast, the least successful, in a deprived valleys county, had won approval for grants totalling only £22 per head. When the database is complete these figures may need slight modification. Moreover, with approvals continuing, some Local Partnerships that had a slow start are catching up. Nevertheless, we must realize that it would blunt the success of Objective 1 if the very areas that had the greatest need were the least successful because of capacity problems. As with community regeneration, such disparities might require proactive help from WEFO and the National Assembly.

HOW WILL WE KNOW IF STRUCTURAL FUNDS ARE WORKING?

Finally, when we have allocated all the funds and the expenditure has been incurred on schedule, can we be certain that the programme has been a success? Will completed projects actually create the predicted number of permanent, sustainable jobs and will the GDP increase by the predicted amount? One of the saddest features of the transition between the 1994–9 programme and the 2000–6 programme was the sequence of applicants who had won awards in the earlier programme and who now pleaded that unless the funding continued without a break the project would collapse. Yet, a fundamental principle of European Structural Funds is that each project supported by the Funds should be sustainable – that is, they should be self-supporting at the end of the programme.

It is very hard to assess the actual benefits derived from the 1994–9 programmes, partly because so much of the programme carried on after 2000, and partly because there was no proper mechanism for monitoring and evaluation. WEFO has now established an Evaluation Unit, and the Monitoring Committee for Objective 1 has set up a Monitoring Subgroup. (*Quis custodiet ipsos custodes?*) The danger is that the results of such evaluation will appear too late to amend the implementation of the first half of the present programme, but at least it will be able to inform any modifications necessary after the half-stage review.

NOTES

1. There was a sharp increase in the index for the UK when Inner London and Outer London were separated. As GDP is measured at place of work there is a large apparent disparity when people live in one region and work in another. This illustrates the limitations of any index based on GDP per head, but there is little doubt that the UK now has the largest regional discrepancies in GDP per head with, for example, the difference in average GDP between Inner London and Cornwall far greater than between Hamburg and Chemnitz.
2. This is another case where advance warning was given. It appears there was no co-ordination in the definitions of rurality adopted in Objective 1, Objective 2, the Rural Development Plan and Leader III.

REFERENCE

European Union (2001). *Second Report on Economic and Social Cohesion.*

9. THE WEST WALES AND VALLEYS OBJECTIVE 1 PROGRAMME: A PERSONAL NARRATIVE

Peter Midmore

INTRODUCTION

In the brief history of the West Wales and the Valleys Objective 1 programme thus far, it is already clear that there are a number of competing narratives. One, the official political defence, already bears a resemblance to the *ex-post* evaluation legally required of all European-funded programmes, concentrating on (among other issues) jobs created or secured, businesses founded, training courses delivered and their take-up, cubic metres of concrete poured and broadband communications networks implemented. The interpretation and evaluation of these summative aggregate assessments, based on the priorities and measures contained in the Single Programming Document (SPD), follow a well-worn path set out, for example, in the European Commission's own (1999) comprehensive manuals. However, from my own subjective perspective as an actor in the overall process of development and implementation of the Objective 1 programme, albeit with particular specialist knowledge, I do not consider this to be a complete account, or even necessarily an important part of it. Rather, I will argue that adopting this perspective might actually harm the prospects for resilient and useful economic progress in the least advantaged parts of Wales.

The announcement in 1998 that West Wales and the Valleys had been designated an Objective 1 region was received with a surge of consensual enthusiasm. Four years on, although the excitement of that time has faded, a number of disagreements have emerged with the (loosely characterized) official perspective above. These include the question of whether sufficient, genuinely additional funding is being provided by the Treasury (Bristow and Blewitt, 1999); the need for greater urgency to get the money flowing towards the most acute economic problems of the Objective 1 region;[1] and whether an almost entirely unified programme without significant spatial targeting is appropriate to the enormous diversity of the Objective 1 region (Brooksbank et al., 2001). Whilst these are all legitimate matters of contention, none really gets to the core of the far more difficult and complex issue of governance of the programme itself, in particular, securing the engagement of all relevant stakeholders in the current programme to achieve its maximum impact.

The main aim of this article is to examine, in more detail, the flaws in this conspiracy of official optimism about the Objective 1 programme. The following section briefly discusses means and ends in regional economic policy. This prepares the ground for the next section exploring a more critical perspective on current efforts in West Wales and the Valleys. The final section provides some concluding commentary on policy implications, and what, if anything, might be done differently in the remaining four years of the programme.

MEANS AND ENDS IN REGIONAL ECONOMIC POLICY

The danger inherent in using indicators of economic development is that, if a measurement becomes a target of policy, the underlying phenomenon it is supposed to assess itself often undergoes a subtle shift.[2] Paradoxically, that seems to make such measures less useful as guides to performance than they were before they became targets. Thus, indicator-driven policy implementation concentrates attention on the means to regional development as if they were the ends, and thus tends to neglect fundamental processes and causal relationships; increases in employment, increasing levels of investment in technology and technological competence are a reflection of successful development, rather than the cause of it.

One of the products of this confusion, reflected in the elegant and intelligent prose of the civil servants whose job is to defend and promote the current wisdom, is essentially a closed vision. For example, *A Winning Wales* (NAW, 2002a) sets out a tightly constructed standpoint which appears to have assessed all relevant problems, assembles an optimum set of responses within the limits of feasible action, and thus disposes of the need for any further thinking. In broader terms, *A Winning Wales* simply reflects the standard regional development approach applied more or less everywhere in the club of rich nations in the Organization for Economic Cooperation and Development (OECD). Yet all the available evidence suggests that, in an increasingly globalized world, deviation from the norm, especially with respect to creativity, is one of the most important indicators of successful performance of regions (see, for example, IWA, 2001; Hassink and Lagendijk, 2001).

To develop a narrative more reflective of the bottom-up realities of the Objective 1 programme, we need to cultivate a richer conception of the economy, as an alternative to the dominant, reductionist, 'black box' paradigm. This latter perspective focuses chiefly on the conversion of inputs into outputs, on increasing the margin between the two, and on equitably distributing the surplus between factor incomes due to labour, capital and entrepreneurship. It badly needs to be augmented by greater sociological understanding of the fact that the economy is also a network of relation-ships between individuals inhabiting real institutions, embedded in a culture of shared history, identity and confidence; and also that exchanges across this network themselves influence behaviour, both individually and collectively. Policy-makers and policy-implementers, though the mode and intensity of their interaction may be dissimilar, are as involved in this network as any other participant; the myth of dualism in which the policy-makers act somehow outside and objectively on the subject of the regional economy is damaging in the extreme. If they aspire (as most do) to establish a learning region, then this network (including them as integral elements) must itself engage in policy learning, as much as attempting to promote innovation and entrepreneurship (Benz and Furst, 2002).

The rhetoric policy-makers employ (unfortunately and also partly coincidentally) portrays policy implementation as external, objective, and capable of being evaluated from the same detached viewpoint. However, if it can be accepted that it is not possible to separate the means by which policy is delivered from the experience of participating in the reality as a whole, then a different story emerges. My own relatively limited involvement in both the process of policy development and implementation forms the basis, in the next section, for the alternative story so far of the Objective 1 pro-gramme. This perspective is not entirely straightforward, or disingenuous, since I have fairly well-established academic interests in regional and rural development (for example, Midmore, 1998). However, having declared these subjective biases in advance, the purpose of the narrative which emerges is essentially to contribute to the development of dialogue and debate and, if successful, ultimately to improve policy development itself. Though subjective, provided it resonates with the perspective of other participants in the process, that in itself is justification for exploring the questions it raises further. If it is not provided with broad confirmation, then at least there is scope for clarification which may eventually help to resolve the many anxieties being expressed about the programme as a whole.

KEY EVENTS: WALES AND OBJECTIVE 1

A recent policy statement on higher education (NAW, 2002b: 12) 'greatly values developing links with the sector to increase its evidence base', and it does seem sensible that academics should contribute any relevant expertise to policy-making in their own localities. Perhaps even more importantly, it also presents an opportunity to develop practical understanding, as a counterweight to treasured theoretical paradigms. In view of that, from 1997 to 1999, I served as the member of the Rural Wales Objective 5b Programme Monitoring Committee representing higher education. During the early part of my term, the prospects of achieving Objective 1 status for Wales seemed distant, and, in retrospect, it all happened very quickly: first, the NUTS 2 boundaries were redrawn, then Eurostat's calculations showed that GDP in West Wales and the Valleys was 73 per cent of the EU average, and from that point it became ultimately inevitable that Objective One status would be achieved. Only then, however (and probably far too late) did the substantive work on developing a Single Programming Document (SPD) begin. Hywel Ceri Jones's Task Force was established in 1998 once official confirmation of the Objective 1 process was made, and, as part of that, I became a member of the Academic Advisory Socio-Economic Panel, one of the many and diverse groups that were initiated to feed into the process of developing consensus.

Two major incidents stand out in my memory of this period. The first was a seminar held in Cardiff in January 1999, involving broad stakeholder representation, which made significant advances towards producing a draft SPD. It took place over two days and provided extensive opportunities for discussion between a broad range of public, voluntary and (to a lesser extent) private sector interests. The second event was less auspicious. In the summer of the same year, the Task Force was summarily disbanded and consultants were hired instead to produce a SPD more acceptable to the European Commission, whose power to withhold approval (technically, co-decision) could put back the whole programme.

The latter event can be defended as an urgent and necessary step in securing the prize of a sizeable investment injection, or as action born of an anxiety to avoid delays in implementation. Yet, for many, it had the shock effect of dissolving any illusions about the supposed partnership approach, particularly among those of us outside the charmed circle of the National Assembly and its principal sponsored public bodies.

To complete the story, today in theory at least, I am a nominal member or adviser to a number of regional, local and sectoral partnerships in various hierarchical relationships to the overall Programme Monitoring Committee. Firstly, like many others in a similar situation, my successful participation in any one can only occur to the detriment of involvement in all of the others: in fact, it is impossible to do justice to them all.[3] Secondly, this lack of streamlining enormously favours the professional members of the partnerships, who have specialist insider access to resources and networks enabling them to manage discussion to their advantage, which has led to dismay among those outside the policy loop. Pressures are particularly acute for representatives of voluntary organizations and private sector interests, and because of poor transport links and sparsity of population, also discriminate against rural as opposed to urban interests. Therefore, it is unsurprising that participation by the business community in the Objective 1 programme has been desultory, thus far, because it has become viewed as a stitch-up between the National Assembly, the Welsh Development Agency and local government. Correspondingly, this also explains why the majority of commitments under the programme have been on public sector projects which, whilst ostensibly providing improvements to the climate of business opportunity, in reality consolidate the influence and resources of the state institutions.

Combined, the consequences of all this have the effect of diluting and diminishing the social capital which, although as fundamental to economic regeneration as physical infrastructure and incentives, is not easily measurable and is therefore often ignored (Putnam, 1993). This leads to a discussion of fundamental issues in regional economic development, and the importance of concentrating on the quality of partnerships to achieve objectives.

Often regional development objectives are portrayed as either improving economic efficiency, and therefore fully employing spatially diverse resources, or addressing economic inequities through space (for example, Armstrong and Taylor, 2000). However, a focus on one of these outcomes neglects the role of process in achieving either; in fact, in both, many commentators concur with my personal reflection that the quality of social capital *specific to the policy community* critically determines the effectiveness of policy impact. Whilst social capital revolves around the concepts of trust (deriving from the New Institutional Economics concern with reduction in transactions and administrative costs) and associability (improving the stochastic likelihood of coincidentally mutually beneficial interaction between public and private sectors), more recent discussions have emphasized the critical role of central governments (in Wales, the role played by the National Assembly) in promoting what is termed 'institutional thickness' (Amin and Thrift, 1994).

In practice, there is a relative absence in Wales of the kind of network between people and institutions involved in regional development processes. Such networks help to smooth the passage of implementation, but they take time to establish and nurture: MacLeod (2001: 1145) suggests that their neglect reflects a ' . . . failure to appreciate fully the crucial role of the state in shaping the urban-regional process, and a related weakness in examining the asymmetries of power which enframe the governance of space economies'. However, if this diagnosis is accepted by policy-makers, there then emerges a conflict between the rather more open, exploratory and facilitating role it implies and the significantly different traditional public face of governmentality, designed to defend authority and competence. It is, however, possible to decentralize responsibility so that a broader range of participants can use alternative organizational frameworks and information resources to improve the effectiveness of regional interventions (Halkier, 2001), and there is a continuing, if transformed, role for the state as a regulator of activities. At present, whilst there is some limited participation in policy implementation, the state retains overall control, acting as a so-called 'gatekeeper' by intervening at all levels of the policy process (Bache, 1999).

CHOICES FOR ACTORS IN THE OBJECTIVE 1 SETTING

This personal narrative has highlighted the importance of social capital in the regional economic development process; there is now an accumulating literature demonstrating its critical importance in the overall mixture of influences which contribute to 'successful' regions. It is, of course, also important as an end in its own right, as it contributes significantly to quality of life; the greater the number of people there are able to contribute effectively to decision-making processes, the more likely it is that locally appropriate decisions are taken, whilst at the same time sufficient civic culture will accumulate to ensure that issues affecting broader interests can be dealt with sympathetically. However, social capital only accumulates little by little, deriving from collective experiences in relation to culture, religion, history and shared identity: it is therefore difficult to generate through public policy actions although, as I hope I have demonstrated, easy to diminish without realizing, since it does give rise to problems of recognition and measurement (Higgs and White, 2001).

The perspective I have developed recognizes that all actors in the policy process are embedded in the same network, and draw on a common stock of social capital which some are 'privileged' to deplete more rapidly than others. This helps to explain more clearly the divergence between a business-friendly rhetoric in regional policy and a reality of increased power in the insider networks of regional administration. Ultimately, the strength of this discourse may provide a satisfactory account of the management of the Objective 1 programme, through conventional evaluation methodologies. In due course also, however, an opportunity to develop networks and synergy-focused interactions will not have been fully exploited. Because the Structural Funds Programmes now form the predominant channel for regional public assistance in the United Kingdom, as elsewhere in the EU, the various partnerships and monitoring arrangements constitute the chief arena for stakeholder interaction. The tone set by the 1999 decision to rely on external experts rather than stakeholders to finalize the SPD and the subsequent management of the programme have thus had critical effects.

Nonetheless, the choices now available for actors in the current round of policies in the period 2000–5 are limited. The administrative machinery of implementation has not been designed to respond flexibly to the changing perceptions of all participants in the Objective 1 programme, which is why for practical purposes the narrative begins and ends so abruptly in 1999. Clearly, however, there is a longer-term problem which will eventually have to be addressed, whose solution involves a change to the culture of the state institutions themselves. Fundamentally, this involves a more intelligent and subtle interaction by the National Assembly and its strategic sponsored public bodies, particularly involving greater self-restraint in order to promote the more efficient use of their resources and influence. That will require patience in the face of the frustrations that inevitably arise when acting more openly and sensitively to the needs of stakeholders outside the charmed circles of regional and local government. However, such sustained efforts, within the framework of the remaining period of the Objective 1 programme, constitute the best available approach first to conserve, and then gradually to extend, the relevant social capital for improved regional development. For those of us who are outside, the best we can do is to encourage the insiders to act in this manner.

NOTES

1. To be fair, the contrary view is that there are necessary checks on the expenditure of large amounts of public money which, since the potential for substantial public aid for regional development from any source beyond 2006 is limited, is a one-off opportunity which it is essential to get right. It is worth noting that the spending of the programme can only be limited in its effect, unless it is used strategically or catalytically to lever more substantial impact; otherwise, £1.3 billion over six years from EU sources, matched by national government sources, might be enough in round terms, to give each inhabitant the yearly equivalent of a Building Society demutualization bonus. Also, establishing the apparatus to administer the programme equitably and legitimately, with appropriate representation and gender balance, in such a short time is a substantial achievement. Perhaps it is more remarkable for not taking longer to set up.

2. This tendency is often referred to as 'Goodhart's Law', which although originally applied to financial assets (Goodhart, 1984), has been generalized to suggest that when any measure becomes a target, it ceases to be a good measure: for further discussion, see Hoskin (1996).

3. Although du Gay (2000), writing in praise of bureaucracy, redresses important imbalances in perception concerning administrative processes and their social importance, this defence can be taken too far!

REFERENCES

Amin, A. and Thrift, N. (eds) (1994). *Globalization, Institutions, and Regional Development in Europe*, Oxford and New York, Oxford University Press.

Armstrong, H. and Taylor, J. (2000). *Regional Economics and Policy*, 3rd edn, Malden, MA, Blackwell Publishers.

Bache, I. (1999). 'The extended gatekeeper: central government and the implementation of EC regional policy in the UK', *Journal of European Public Policy*, 6 (1), 28–45.

Benz, A. and Furst, D. (2002). 'Policy learning in regional networks', *European Urban and Regional Studies*, 9 (1), 21–35.

Bristow, G. and Blewitt, N. (1999). *Unravelling The Knot: The Interaction of UK Treasury and European Union Funding for Wales*, Institute of Welsh Affairs Research Report, Cardiff, IWA.

Brooksbank, D. J., Clifton, N. C., Jones-Evans, D. and Pickernell, D. G. (2001). 'The end of the beginning? Welsh regional policy and Objective One', *European Planning Studies*, 9 (2), 255–74.

European Commission (1999). *MEANS Collection: Evaluating Socio-economic Programmes*, Luxembourg, Office for Official Publications of the European Communities.

du Gay, P. (2000). *In Praise of Bureaucracy: Weber, Organization, Ethics*, London, Sage.

Goodhart, C. A. E. (1984). *Monetary Theory and Practice: The UK Experience*, London, Macmillan.

Halkier, H. (2001). 'Regional policy in transition: a multi-level governance perspective on the case of Denmark', *European Planning Studies*, 9 (3), 323–38.

Hassink, R. and Lagendijk, A. (2001). 'The dilemmas of interregional institutional learning', *Environment and Planning C – Government and Policy*, 19 (1), 65–84.

Higgs, G. and White, S. (2001). 'Using measures of social capital to monitor the impacts of community-led regeneration policies in Wales', *Contemporary Wales*, 14, 144–63.

Hoskin, K. (1996). 'The "awful idea of accountability": inscribing people into the measurement of objects', in Munro, R. and Mouritsen, J. (eds), *Accountability: Power, Ethos and the Technologies of Managing*, London, International Thomson Business Press, 265–82.

Institute of Welsh Affairs (2001). *World Best Practice in Regional Economic Development*, Cardiff, IWA.

MacLeod, G. (2001). 'Beyond soft institutionalism: accumulation, regulation, and their geographical fixes', *Environment and Planning A*, 33 (7), 1145–67.

Midmore, P. (1998). 'Rural policy reform and local development programmes: appropriate evaluation procedures', *Journal of Agricultural Economics*, 49 (3), 407–24.

National Assembly for Wales (NAW) (2002a). *A Winning Wales: The National Economic Development Strategy of the Welsh Assembly Government*, Cardiff, NAW.

National Assembly for Wales (NAW) (2002b). *Reaching Higher: Higher Education and the Learning Country*, Cardiff, NAW.

Putnam, R. D. (1993). *Making Democracy Work: Civic Traditions in Modern Italy*, Princeton, N.J. and Chichester, Princeton University Press.

10. CONSTITUENCY CAMPAIGNING IN WALES AT THE 2001 GENERAL ELECTION

David Denver and Iain MacAllister*

Constituency campaigning is a traditional and familiar aspect of general elections in Britain. In the weeks leading up to the election, posters are displayed, candidates 'press the flesh', leaflets are handed out in the street or delivered to voters' homes, party workers canvass the electorate and so on. On polling day itself the parties mount 'get out the vote' operations. Until recently, however, academics and commentators paid little attention to local campaigning and even the parties appeared more concerned to ensure that their election broadcasts were well produced, that leading figures performed well on television and that they had an effective national media strategy than they were with the quality of campaigning on the ground.

Over the last decade, however, there has been a renewal of interest in, and revaluation of, the impact of constituency campaigning on election outcomes. In general, the parties have taken constituency campaigning much more seriously. In parallel, a significant 'revisionist' literature has emerged arguing that constituency campaigning has become much more sophisticated and that variations in the effectiveness and intensity of constituency campaigning give rise to variations in party performance. The better the local campaign, the better the local result (see, for example, Denver and Hands, 1997; Denver et al., forthcoming, 2002).

Thus far this literature has focused entirely on Britain as a whole. This is understandable, but it means that distinctive elements of electoral politics and of the electoral context in Wales are effectively ignored. Most obviously, perhaps, little attention has been paid to campaigning by Plaid Cymru, even though the party obviously plays a significant part in Welsh electoral politics (coming third in terms of vote share, with 14.3 per cent in 2001). Moreover, the significant presence of Plaid means that patterns of party competition at constituency level are more varied and more complicated than is the case in most English seats. In addition, it seems likely that campaigning in Wales will be affected by the fact that Welsh seats are more rural than those in England. Only six of the forty Welsh seats are very or mainly urban while this is true of more than half (53 per cent) of English constituencies. The electoral status of Welsh seats, a factor which critically affects the strength of campaigns, also differs markedly from those in England. Going into the 2001 election, about two-thirds of constituencies in Wales were very safe for Labour in general election terms while about 85 per cent were hopeless prospects for the Conservatives. In England, about 40 per cent of seats fell into each of these categories.

Finally, devolution has made for a marked change in the electoral context of campaigning. It was always the case that all of the British-wide parties devolved considerable autonomy to their Welsh headquarters. Specifically Welsh campaign themes would be developed, for example, and Welsh-orientated election literature produced. As usual, this again occurred in the 2001 general election (see Mitchell and Bradbury, 2002). As far as constituency campaigning was concerned, however, before devolution the strategies to be pursued were generally laid down by the parties' London headquarters and implemented with relatively minor changes in Wales. In 2001, however, the parties had to take into account the Welsh National Assembly elections in 1999 and also have in mind plans for campaigning in the next round of Assembly elections in 2003. In addition, the establishment of the Assembly indirectly provided a potential boost to campaigning. Members of the Assembly have been able to appoint staff to work for them and in the general election these employees could be diverted (whether on paid leave or not) to work in the campaign. Since most would be experienced and able to work full-time on campaigning, this could have had an impact on the quality and effectiveness of at least some constituency campaigns.

PARTY STRATEGIES FOR CONSTITUENCY CAMPAIGNING IN 2001

In strategic terms all parties now recognize that in planning and executing constituency campaigns targeting is the name of the game. Under the first-past-the-post electoral system, most seats are either safe or hopeless for one party or another (mostly safe for Labour in Wales) and there is, therefore, little to be gained from campaigning strongly in these seats. Rather, all parties attempt to target effort and resources into a relatively small number of key seats where there is a possibility that they might gain the seat from the incumbent or lose it to a challenger. The aim is to mount the best possible campaigns in the constituencies where effective campaigning might make a difference to the outcome.

Labour's national strategy in respect of constituency campaigning in 2001 was called Operation Turnout and any constituency could opt into the programme of activity that was prescribed. In practice, however, attention nationally was focused on 148 'priority' seats, all but two of which had been gained in 1997 and of which seven were in Wales. From the perspective of Welsh Labour, however, things would have looked rather different. Results from our post-election postal survey of election agents suggest that two of the seats on the national target list (Preseli Pembrokeshire and Vale of Clwyd) were not given a high priority within Wales. This is not difficult to understand as these were only 'notional' gains in 1997 following extensive boundary revisions and had actually been won very comfortably. In addition, Labour had been given a real shock in the Assembly elections in 1999, losing five seats to Plaid and one each to the Conservatives and the Liberal Democrats. Some of these had previously been considered very safe and it seems certain that these would have been targeted by Welsh Labour in 2001 in an attempt to restore the party's position. This suggestion is again supported by survey returns from election agents.

Following devolution, the main focus of Plaid Cymru's concerns shifted from the House of Commons to the National Assembly for Wales. This impression was heightened by the fact that three of the party's four MPs had stood down in order to concentrate on the Assembly. The Plaid leadership, therefore, had to convince activists and electors alike that the party still considered the House of Commons important. In addition, the party faced something of a dilemma over whether to concentrate on trying to win seats in the general election or on consolidating and preparing the ground for the next Assembly elections. Nonetheless, the situation with respect to the targeting of constituencies by Plaid is clear. Party officials indicated in interviews that attention was focused on the four seats held in 1997 and the five 'gained' from Labour in 1999. Telephone canvassing of voters in these seats was undertaken both from party headquarters and in the constituencies themselves, with well over 100,000 calls being made.

Nationally, the Conservatives began their preparations for the 2001 campaign with a long list of 180 target seats – all of them seats in which the party was challenging the incumbent – of which nine were in Wales. It seems clear, however, that some of the party's more distant prospects were placed on the target list more in hope than expectation and that, in practice, attention was increasingly concentrated on a smaller number, especially since opinion polls failed to detect any significant shift of opinion in favour of the Conservatives either in the months before the election or during the campaign itself. It seems likely that, in the end, only five Welsh seats could be considered serious targets for the Conservatives.

After the 1997 general election the Liberal Democrats held two seats in Wales. One of these (Montgomeryshire) is among their safest in Britain but the other (Brecon and Radnorshire) has been very marginal historically and was one of their targets. The only other Welsh seat in which the Liberal Democrats were within hailing distance of the winner was Cardiff Central. They won this seat in the Assembly election and so it was their second target seat.

Our categorization of target seats for each of the parties in Wales is shown in Table 10.1.

TABLE **10.1**
Target seats in Wales

Conservatives	Labour	Lib Dem	Plaid Cymru
Brecon & Radnorshire	Clwyd West	Brecon & Radnorshire	Carmarthen East &
Cardiff North	Cardiff Central	Cardiff Central	Dinefwr
Clwyd West	Cardiff North		Conwy
Monmouth	Carmarthen East &		Islwyn
Vale of Glamorgan	Dinefwr		Llanelli
	Conwy		Rhondda
	Islwyn		Caernarfon
	Llanelli		Ceredigion
	Monmouth		Meirionnydd Nant
	Rhondda		Conwy
	Vale of Glamorgan		Ynys Môn

CONSTITUENCY CAMPAIGNING IN 2001

On the basis of surveys of election agents at the last three general elections, Denver and Hands have developed various indexes measuring the intensity of the campaigns fought by the parties in constituencies (for details see Denver et al., forthcoming, 2002). When the most recent index is computed for the 2001 election, on the basis of all responses across Britain, the mean scores for each party in Wales, as compared with England and Scotland, were as shown in Table 10.2. On this index, a campaign of average intensity scores 100.

The overall scores for each nation show that the strongest constituency campaigns were fought in England, with a score of 102, while the weakest campaigns, on average, were in Wales, with a score of 89, considerably below the mean of 100 for Great Britain as a whole. It might be thought, as suggested above, that relatively weak campaigning in Wales reflected the fact that proportionately there are many more safe Labour seats in Wales than in England, but the detailed figures for the different parties show that this is not the case. Labour's campaigns in Wales were stronger than in other parts of Britain and by far the strongest within Wales. On the other hand, Conservative and Liberal Democrat campaigns were weaker than in England, which is not surprising given that there were very few Welsh constituencies where they had reasonable prospects of success. Plaid Cymru campaigns were also relatively weak compared with campaigns across Britain – slightly weaker, indeed, than Scottish National Party (SNP) campaigns in Scotland.

TABLE 10.2
Mean overall campaign intensity by party and nation

	Wales	England	Scotland	Great Britain
Conservative	88	119	88	114
Labour	111	109	104	108
Liberal Democrats	69	82	70	80
Plaid Cymru	88	–	–	91
SNP	–	–	91	88
Overall	89	102	91	100

Note: The numbers of cases on which the figures are based are as follows: Wales: Conservative 18, Labour 29, Liberal Democrat 25, Plaid Cymru 27; England: Conservative 315, Labour 368, Liberal Democrat 359; Scotland: Conservative 42, Labour 46, Liberal Democrat 48, SNP 52.

For the purposes of this article, however, we have recalculated the index of campaign intensity on the basis of responses from Welsh constituencies only. Of the forty Welsh seats, responses were obtained from eighteen Conservative agents, twenty-nine Labour, twenty-five Liberal Democrat and twenty-seven Plaid Cymru, giving an overall response rate of 61.9 per cent. Subsequent analysis is based on these responses.

A simple indicator of the amount of campaigning going on in a constituency is the number of party workers involved during the campaign and on polling day. Although campaigning has been modernized through the use of computers and telephones, parties still need volunteers on the ground to deliver leaflets, canvass, check off people as they vote and knock up the tardy. Table 10.3 shows the mean numbers of party workers involved on a typical campaign day and on polling day in Welsh constituencies, categorized on the basis of their target status for each party. Unfortunately, we had only one response from a Conservative target and one from a Liberal Democrat target; in addition, all Plaid-held seats were targeted by the party. This limits the extent to which we can make comparisons across parties and seat categories.

Nonetheless, it is clear that all parties had a relatively small number of campaign workers in their weakest seats (not held, not targeted). Labour and Plaid had most in their targets although the former had almost as many in their safe seats. On polling day the same broad pattern was repeated. Overall, Labour had most people on the ground both during the campaign and on polling day, with the Conservatives and Plaid vying for second place. To the extent that the evidence from just one seat in each case is meaningful, the data suggest that the Conservatives and Liberal Democrats did concentrate their election workers in their key seats, especially on polling day.

TABLE **10.3**
Mean number of campaign and polling day workers

	Non-target Held	Target	Non-target Not held	All
Campaign Workers				
Conservative	–	75	18	21
Labour	41	46	16	38
Lib Dem	35	30	12	14
Plaid Cymru	–	38	14	20
Polling Day Workers				
Conservative	–	200	17	27
Labour	77	106	22	74
Lib Dem	50	100	8	14
Plaid Cymru	–	73	16	31

Note: The numbers on which the figures here and in the relevant part of Table 10.4 are based are: for non-target held: Labour 17, Liberal Democrats 1; for targets: Conservative 1, Labour 7, Liberal Democrats 1, Plaid Cymru 7; for non-targets not held: Conservative 17, Labour 5, Liberal Democrats 23, Plaid Cymru 20.

We asked election agents in our survey whether they received volunteers from other constituencies on polling day or sent volunteers to work in other seats. Of the seven Labour target seats in our survey, three reported that activists from other constituencies helped on polling day as did two of the seven Plaid targets. The single Conservative target also received volunteers but the Liberal Democrat target did not (perhaps on account of geographical remoteness). From the other perspective, only one of seventeen Conservative non-target constituencies sent volunteers to key seats, as compared with twelve of twenty-two Labour non-targets, thirteen of twenty-four Liberal Democrat non-targets and six of twenty Plaid non-targets. Labour, it seems, was the most successful party in moving workers to key constituencies. On the other hand, in a curious parallel with the SNP in Scotland, which has a similar problem, this is an aspect of constituency campaigning about which Plaid Cymru appears to have a bit to learn, although it would be difficult to direct workers to their targets in north and west Wales.

There is much more to constituency campaigning than having workers on the ground, of course. The numbers of workers tell us nothing, for example, about the extent of telephone canvassing, now considered a key campaign technique. For a fuller measure of campaign intensity and effort, we return to the index of campaigning mentioned above but this time present the results which are obtained when only Welsh constituencies are used to construct the index. Table 10.4 shows figures for overall campaign strength for each party in different types of seat on the basis of this 'Welsh-only' index. In this case an average campaign *in Wales* scores 100.

The first row shows the scores for all constituencies and it can be seen that, overall, Labour had the strongest constituency campaigns in Wales in 2001, followed by Plaid and the Conservatives, whose campaigns were just below the Welsh average, with the Liberal Democrats lagging well behind. The second part of the table focuses on the well-known 'Three Wales' categorization which distinguishes *Y Fro Gymraeg* (Welsh-speaking areas of north and west Wales), 'Welsh Wales' (broadly the south Wales valleys) and 'British Wales' (the border counties, the south west and the south-east strip from the English border to Cardiff). The Conservatives and Labour clearly campaigned hardest in the latter, although Labour campaigns were of above average intensity in each of the three areas. Plaid Cymru, on the other hand, mounted the strongest campaigns of all in its Welsh-speaking heartlands. Both Plaid and the Liberal Democrats had their poorest campaigns in 'Welsh Wales' which is, of course, largely dominated by Labour.

TABLE 10.4

Campaign intensity scores (Wales)

	Conservative	Labour	Liberal Democrat	Plaid Cymru	All
All	97	123	77	98	100
'Three Wales' category					
Y Fro Gymraeg	89	116	80	144	108
Welsh Wales	90	113	69	69	91
British Wales	107	132	81	81	103
Winner 1997					
Labour	99	132	71	92	100
Liberal Democrat	114	81	129	–	108
Plaid Cymru	79	84	83	145	98
Target status					
Held not target	–	119	112	–	119
Target	151	162	146	138	150
Not held not target	94	83	73	84	83

Note: The numbers involved in the 'Three Wales' category are: *Y Fro Gymraeg*: Conservative 5, Labour 5, Liberal Democrat 5, Plaid Cymru 5; Welsh Wales: Conservative 5, Labour 9, Liberal Democrat 8, Plaid Cymru 9; British Wales: Conservative 8, Labour 15, Liberal Democrat 12, Plaid Cymru 13.

The numbers in the Winner 1997 category are: Labour held: Conservative 13, Labour 24, Liberal Democrat 20, Plaid Cymru 24; Liberal Democrat held: Conservative 2, Labour 2, Liberal Democrat 2; Plaid Cymru held: Conservative 3, Labour 3, Liberal Democrat 3, Plaid Cymru 3.

Also shown in the table are campaign strength scores in constituencies won by the different parties in 1997. Labour had its strongest campaigns – and stronger than those of any other party – in seats that it already held, while it was well below average in other seats. This is not surprising given the essentially defensive strategy adopted by Labour. The aim was to hold what had been won in 1997 and repel the threat posed by Plaid Cymru following the latter's success in the Assembly elections. Although the number of cases is small, Plaid and the Liberal Democrats also fought their strongest campaigns in seats that they held, while Conservative campaigning was strongest in Liberal Democrat seats.

The most important part of Table 10.4, however, relates to the target status of constituencies. As discussed above, the objective of party strategists is now to concentrate campaign resources in a relatively small number of target seats. Although the evidence for the Conservatives and Liberal Democrats must be treated with caution, the data in the table suggest that this aim was achieved by all parties. We can be more confident about the figures for Labour and Plaid and it can be seen that Labour's campaigns were strongest by far in their targets (average score 162), relatively strong in safe seats (119) and below the average intensity for Wales in seats that were not held and not targeted (83). Similarly, Plaid campaigns were much stronger in targets (138) than elsewhere (84). Like Labour and Plaid, the strength of Conservative and Liberal Democrat campaigns were below the Welsh average in seats that were not held and not targeted (scoring 94 and 73 respectively).

THE ELECTORAL IMPACT OF CONSTITUENCY CAMPAIGNING

It is clear, then, that the intensity or strength of the campaigns mounted by the parties varies a great deal across constituencies. In Wales, among our respondents, the index of campaigning for the Conservatives ranged from 52 to 151. For Labour the range was from 65 to 184 (the strongest campaign of all), for the Liberal Democrats 55 (the weakest of all) to 146 and for Plaid Cymru from 58 to 154. The question is, however, whether these sorts of variations are associated with variations in the electoral performance of the party concerned. Across British constituencies as a whole in 2001, for all three British-wide parties, variations in campaign strength were significantly associated with variations in electoral performance (see Denver et al., forthcoming, 2002). The better the constituency campaign, the better the party's performance. Here we consider the question in relation to variations within Wales and include Plaid Cymru in the analysis.

Analysing the electoral impact of variations in campaigning is not straightforward. Indeed, it involves some quite complicated statistics. Without going into technical details, we have undertaken a series of regression analyses in which the share of the electorate obtained in 2001 by the relevant party is the dependent variable, with share obtained in 1997 and score on the campaigning index as the independent variables. The results tell us what difference campaigning made to the share of the electorate obtained, once share in 1997 is taken into account. The coefficients for the campaigning index are shown in Table 10.5.

On a technical note, it should be said that the level of statistical significance found in analyses of this kind depends partly on the numbers of cases involved and, with only eighteen to twenty-nine cases here, statistically significant effects in Wales alone will inevitably be rarer than in analyses involving all British constituencies, for which our numbers vary between 374 and 442. The regression results show that in Wales the level of Conservative campaigning was not associated with variations in the party's performance as compared with 1997. The coefficient for the Liberal Democrats is in the anticipated direction – stronger campaigns were associated with better results – but again this is not a statistically significant result. In the cases of Labour and Plaid Cymru, however, the results are statistically significant (at the 10 per cent level – and almost at the more stringent 5 per cent level) and show that variations in the intensity of their campaigns were positively associated with variations in their electoral performance. The better these parties' campaigns, the better they did in the election.

Table 10.5
Campaign intensity (Welsh) and party performance

	Conservative	Labour	Liberal Democrat	Plaid Cymru
Campaign Intensity Index	–0.144	**2.96**	3.64	**4.04**

Notes: The figures shown are unstandardized regression coefficients which, for ease of presentation, have been multiplied by 100. Statistically significant coefficients (p < 0.10) are printed in bold. Numbers of cases are: Conservative 18, Labour 29, Liberal Democrat 25, Plaid Cymru 27.

To give some more straightforward idea of the size of these effects, the coefficient for Labour campaigning implies that, having taken account of the party's share of the electorate in 1997, a campaign typical of their weakest third (score 88) would have increased their share of the electorate in 2001 by 2.6 percentage points, while one typical of their strongest third (score 162) would have increased the share by 4.8 percentage points. The respective figures for Plaid are 2.7 points and 5.4 points. The differences between the effects of weak and strong campaigning are not enormous, of course, but they would not be expected to be very large as constituency campaigning is only one of many factors affecting election results. Voters are obviously influenced by the national context of elections – national leaders, issues, party images and so on – as well as the local context. There are national trends and tides, and constituency campaigning can usually serve only to stem or accentuate them in particular instances. In Wales in 2001, Labour and Plaid managed to do this.

CONCLUSION

The different context in which elections in Wales are fought makes a difference to the pattern of constituency campaigning. Targeting strategies in 2001 reflected not only party strengths in the previous general election but also the constituency results in the first Welsh Assembly elections in 1999; they involved not only the calculations of party strategists in London but also those of the Welsh leadership in Cardiff. Unsurprisingly, Labour has the strongest campaigns overall, but Plaid are by far the most intense campaigners in north and west Wales. Given that they hold no seats, the campaigns mounted by the Conservatives are, perhaps surprisingly, strong and it would seem that they campaign particularly strongly in the few seats where they have a chance of winning. Apart from two or three seats, Liberal Democrat campaigning is weak.

Despite our analysis being hampered by the small numbers of constituencies involved, we have shown that Labour and Plaid Cymru campaigning had an electoral pay-off. Both did better where they campaigned more strongly. An improvement of around 2 per cent of the electorate achieved by stronger campaigning may seem like a small return for the effort involved. This translates into a greater proportion of the votes cast, however, and in close contests could well make the difference between winning and losing.

*The research on which this article is based was supported by the ESRC (grant reference number R000239 396).

REFERENCES

Denver, D. and Hands, G. (1997). *Modern Constituency Electioneering*, London, Frank Cass.

Denver, D., Hands, G., Fisher, J. and MacAllister, I. (forthcoming, 2002). 'The impact of constituency campaigning in the 2001 general election', *British Elections and Parties Review*, 12.

Mitchell, J. and Bradbury, J. (2002). 'Scotland and Wales: the first post-devolution general election', in Geddes, A. and Tonge, J. (eds), *Labour's Second Landslide: The British General Election 2001*, Manchester: Manchester University Press, 201–18.

11. POLITICAL INSTITUTIONS, POLICY PREFERENCES AND PUBLIC OPINION IN WALES AND BRITTANY[1]

Alistair Cole with J. Barry Jones, John Loughlin, Colin Williams and Alan Storer

The research project from which this article is drawn investigates processes of regional governance in two cognate yet distinctive regions: Wales and Brittany. It is a binary comparison that does not pretend to exhaust the possibilities of other binary or multivariate comparisons. Starting from the premise that the common challenges of regional governance are at least as important as its institutional variations, we engage in three distinct exercises in comparative investigation: at the level of policy communities (through in-depth interviews in the two regions); issue-networks (through a detailed questionnaire); and public opinion (through a mass opinion poll carried out in both regions in July–August 2001).[2] This article presents some important results of the attitudinal surveys carried out in Wales and Brittany in 2001. These findings illustrate what people living in Wales and Brittany think of their regions and how they envisage their future development.

Why compare Wales and Brittany? Before addressing this issue, we need to determine what is the function of comparison. For policy-makers, comparison is bound up with practical politics. Within the policy community, comparison is envisaged primarily in aspirational terms. This process is important, as the National Assembly for Wales is currently working out its diplomatic priorities. The most obvious comparators are those within the UK itself, as the Welsh look with some envy on the Scottish Parliament with its primary legislative and tax-raising powers. Outside of the UK, Welsh policy-makers look to regions such as Catalonia, or to nation states such as Ireland or Denmark as models.[3] These comparisons are sometimes quite unrealistic. Wales compares itself with the Irish Republic or the Scandinavian democracies, but does not yet possess the requisite political sovereignty to make such a comparison meaningful. Unlike Ireland or

Denmark, Wales is not an EU member state. Others look to Spanish regions such as Catalonia, which share a similar model of asymmetrical devolution to that of Wales within the UK. Or, indeed, to German *länder*, which appear as important nodes within the evolving EU multi-layered polity. Or again to Canada, which has institutionalized the bilingual society to which many in Wales aspire. There is obviously much to be said for comparing Wales and Catalonia or a Canadian province. But, whatever their merits, such comparisons are broadly aspirational; they present an idealized vision of what Wales might become. The economic and demographic underpinnings for such comparisons need to be demonstrated in a more rigorous manner than is usually the case.

Our interest as academics is rather different. Through comparison, we seek to illustrate diversity, as well as similarity. The comparisons we seek to draw are multidimensional ones. We are interested in the analytically separate dimensions of national context, regional identity, public policy and popular legitimization. We contrast distinct traditions of territorial administration in France and Britain, but concentrate our attention on two regions – Wales and Brittany – facing many similar structural challenges and strategic choices. Through making comparisons in the area of education and training and language policy management, we seek to identify useful lessons for policy-makers on both sides of the channel. On the basis of successfully commissioned mass opinion surveys in Wales and Brittany, we are able to test the underlying legitimacy of new forms of regional governance.

We have identified the Wales–Brittany pair as being the most appropriate within the overarching context of Franco-British comparisons. We argue that the mix of similarity and difference makes the Wales–Brittany pair excellent for comparative analysis, in terms of their physical location, their population size, their economic activity, their linguistic specificity and – not least – their common historical ties. Of course, there are important institutional differences between the two. The powers of French regions are much weaker than those of the National Assembly for Wales. In this respect, the project starts from a position of qualitative difference between France and Britain. The British union state was always far more flexible than its French unitary counterpart. On balance, however, the UK has more in common with the unitary state tradition than it does with the federal one. This historical dimension of the comparison is deeply important for understanding how the predominant state tradition is perceived in regions with strong identity such as Wales and Brittany. Before considering in some detail our comparative opinion poll findings, we now present the Brittany region within its national context.

A FRENCH REGION WITH A DIFFERENCE: BRITTANY

One of the most distinctive regions of France, Brittany has a strong sense of its specific position within French society (Favereau, 1993; Flatres, 1986; Ford, 1993; Le Bourdonnec, 1996; Le Coadic, 1998; Martray, 1983). Formerly an independent Duchy (from 818 to 1532), then a French province with special prerogatives (1532–1789), reduced for long to being a collection of disparate *départements* before becoming an administrative then political region, modern Brittany is a French region with a difference. Unlike many other French regions, Brittany can look to its past existence as an independent nation state, with an elaborate set of state institutions and founding myths. Though the symbols of statehood have long been repressed, the region retains many distinctive characteristics. The Breton language is the only Celtic language spoken in continental Europe. The enduring symbolic importance of the Roman Catholic religion is ever present physically in the architecture of Breton villages, as well as in higher than average rates of religious practice. The spectacular growth of Breton cultural movements (dance, theatre, costume) is testament to a revival of Breton values and self-consciousness. At a more abstract level, observers have noted the capacity of Breton actors to join forces to promote their common interests and to defend Brittany against attacks from the outside world (Martray, 1983). Breton solidarity can also be gauged more intuitively by the effectiveness of Breton elite-level networks in Paris and Brussels and by the importance of the Breton diaspora in retaining a sense of distinctiveness.

The dominant political culture is one of political accommodation. Breton politicians of all parties, however divided they are internally, will tend to close ranks against threats from the outside. Despite a strong regional identity, however, Brittany has not produced significant regionalist parties, or at least parties which have been capable of winning seats in departmental, regional or national elections. Only one left-wing regionalist party, the Union Démocratique Bretonne (UDB), has managed some victories at the municipal level and then usually in collaboration with the Socialist Party (PS). Le Coadic (1998) interprets this phenomenon as a consequence of the deeply rooted legitimist strand within Breton public opinion. Imbued by a Catholic, conformist ethic, the Breton public is not prepared to support pro-independence or pro-autonomist parties. We should also note that the mainstream political parties in Brittany have adopted regionalist themes and are more 'regionalist' than their national counterparts. This is true even of the Gaullist (RPR) president of the Brittany region, Josselin de Rohan, who has a much more 'regionalist' discourse than his RPR colleagues in most of the rest of France. Although Breton regionalism has, at times, been violent, this never reached the levels experienced in Corsica, the Spanish Basque country or Northern Ireland.

Brittany is sometimes taken as a litmus test for the health of regional identity within France. In post-war Brittany, there has been a strong political consensus among the regional elites in favour of enhanced regionalization. From 1950 onwards, Breton actors of all political persuasions co-operated closely in the CELIB (*Comité d'étude et de liaison des intérêts bretons*), the archetype of a post-war regional advocacy coalition. The CELIB could claim the credit for many of the improvements in transport infrastructure in the Brittany region in the 1960s and 1970s. Brittany is probably the most distinctive region in mainland France today. This distinctiveness adds a foresight dimension to the Wales–Brittany comparison. Brittany is the birthplace and driving force of regional political identity (and institutions) in France and, if UK-style devolution ever comes to France, it will un-doubtedly prosper in Brittany more than anywhere else.

WHERE SHOULD DECISIONS BE MADE?

The questions we asked in our comparative opinion polls were general ones attempting to capture the rather different situations in Wales and Brittany. There are differences, of course, between Wales and Brittany. Wales has a fairly long history of administrative decentralization and a recent history of political devolution (Jones and Osmond, 2002; Chaney, Hall and Pithouse, 2001; Marinetto, 2001; McAllister, 2000). Brittany has a history of more limited administrative decentralization and a longer, but weaker, political decentralization (Cole and John, 2001). Before analysing the poll findings in more detail, we now briefly compare and contrast the distinctive features of Welsh devolution and French decentralization.

Wales had a history of administrative devolution from 1964 to 1999, which laid the foundations for a more autonomous form of regional governance. Many areas of public policy were, de facto, managed by Welsh civil servants acting independently of their Whitehall colleagues, with minimal supervision exercised by a secretary of state and two junior ministers. Though subject to the political inconsistencies of UK govern-ments and the sensitivities of successive secretaries of state, civil servants in the Welsh Office were usually left to get on with the serious business of policy implementation. The model of executive devolution contained in the

Government of Wales Act (GWA) of 1998 is heavily imbued with the legacy of the Welsh Office, from the precise functions transferred to the key civil service personnel involved in assuring the transition (Rawlings, 1998; Cole and Storer, 2002).

After the narrowest of victories for the Yes campaign in the 1997 referendum, the Government of Wales Act (1998) created a National Assembly with secondary legislative powers, rather than with primary legislative and budgetary powers as in Scotland. In the Welsh model of executive devolution, there is an implicit division of labour between the devolved and central governments (Rawlings, 2001; Patchett, 2000). The core functions of the state remain with central government. These are defence, taxation, social security, immigration and nationality laws. The Government of Wales Act transfers eighteen fields but there is no precise, constitutionally based division as in a genuine federal system. The Assembly 'has the exact powers of the Secretary of State', though the secretary of state had been part of central government with a voice in cabinet. The powers transferred to the Assembly were those of the old Welsh Office, powers that had evolved in an arbitrary and haphazard manner, usually reflecting different traditions within Whitehall departments. Consistent with the doctrine of parliamentary sovereignty, and the principle of secondary legislative powers, Westminster retains legislative pre-eminence even in transferred areas. Conforming to the traditional local government model, moreover, the Assembly can only act where it has precise statutory responsibilities. It cannot invest itself with new responsibilities, nor can it raise additional sources of finance. It can, however, make primary legislation within secondary legislation (through statutory instruments and circulars), which vests it with a distinct policy formulation role. For one of the architects of devolution, the only advantage of this hybrid and ob-fuscated system was that it helped to deliver devolution to Wales. The Welsh public, apathetic when not antipathetic, would not have accepted a bolder scheme.

However we define devolution in Wales, the Brittany regional council's functions are weaker. The regional institution in France is the result of a long process of what might be called 'creeping institutionalization' as it was gradually (and grudgingly) granted a position in the politico-administrative system alongside the *départements* and the *communes* (Dupoirier, 1998; Nay, 1997; Loughlin and Mazey, 1995). Brittany became an administrative region in the late 1950s, acquiring its own indirectly elected regional authority in 1972. The 1982 decentralization reforms introduced direct elections[4] for the regional councils in 1982 (operational since 1986) and reinforced their policy responsibilities. It is important to stress the limited character of French decentralization and regionalization. The regional institution was established while retaining the longer-established and, in many ways, more powerful *départements*. Large cities and towns had also become powerful levels of sub-national government (Cole and John, 2001). The regions might, therefore, be considered the poor cousins of French subnational government. Decentralization in Brittany (and throughout France) is less overtly linked with territorial identity than in the case of Wales or Scotland. Regional structures do not respect the informal boundaries of France's historic regions. Thus the French Basque country – squeezed into the Midi-Pyrenées region – does not even have its own *département*. Alsace and Lorraine are two separate regions. Historic Brittany has been divided ever since Marshall Petain's decision to remove the Loire-Atlantique *département* (and its capital Nantes) from Brittany in 1941. To allow France's historic regions to exist would be tantamount to admitting the existence of a union state of the UK variety, rather than the French unitary version. Decentralization was not intended to give political recognition to specific 'ethnic' groups within France. The only partial exception to this rule is Corsica which has had a specific statute since 1982.

Decentralization in France was supposed to promote better governance, not to challenge the underlying principles of the French unitary state. There is no real equivalent in Brittany of the National Assembly's capacity to adapt primary Westminster legislation. There *are* examples in the overseas French territories, in New Caledonia and French Polynesia especially. The Matignon agreements, if ever implemented, would give the Corsican Assembly the power to adapt primary legislation and make regulations. Nowhere in mainland France, however, is UK-style devolution yet on the agenda. But the regional councils do have precise legal responsibilities in economic development, secondary education, training, transport and several other fields. Moreover, elected French regions have limited tax-varying powers that are not available to the National Assembly for Wales. They have used their powers ambitiously and are actively seeking new powers. The republican belief that all parts of the French territory must be treated exactly the same is increasingly contested, not least from Breton politicians and public opinion.

Though Wales and Brittany represent distinctive forms of political decentralization, our polling evidence reveals a strong demand in both regions for effective regional political institutions (see Table 11.1).

TABLE **11.1**
Institutional preferences in Wales and Brittany

Q. There is a debate today in France/Wales on the future of decentralization/Devolution. Which one of the following options do you prefer?	Brittany	Wales
Abolish the Regional Council/National Assembly for Wales	2	24
Retain a Regional Council/National Assembly with limited powers	44	24
Create an elected parliament with tax-raising and legislative powers	33	38
An autonomous Brittany/an independent Wales	12	11
Don't know	9	3

How should we interpret these findings? Let us first consider the case of Brittany, where regional institutions are well established. In Brittany, as in Wales, we observe overwhelming support for consolidating or strengthening existing regional institutions. There is virtually no constituency for the *status quo ante*; regional institutions are fully accepted as part of the normal democratic process. Breton opinion is very evenly divided between those satisfied with existing arrangements (44 per cent) and those advocating either an assembly with legislative and tax-raising powers (33 per cent) or an 'autonomous' Brittany (12 per cent). These findings confirm the existence of a Breton regional political consciousness. They leave entirely open the question of whether the Breton public would support a more thoroughgoing regional or federal evolution. This survey question has been asked in no other mainland French region, but the consensus expert view emphasizes the complex pattern of multiple Breton identities and a willingness to envisage more advanced forms of political decentralization than elsewhere in France (Pillet, 2001). As in Wales, the autonomy solution is confined to the margins of the political spectrum, a discovery confirmed by the absence of support for a strong autonomist political movement.

Our poll indicates not only strong support for regional political institutions in Brittany, but also a desire to strengthen the regional over the local, national and European levels in specific areas (notably education, training and language, our fields of policy investigation). Following the annual surveys conducted by the Paris-based think tank, the OIP (Observatoire Interrégional du Politique), these trends are more pronounced in Brittany than elsewhere. This sense of regional ownership is well demonstrated by our Brittany-specific question on the administrative reunification of the historic Brittany region. Historic Brittany consisted of five *départements,* stretching from the far western Atlantic coast to the Loire. During the wartime authoritarian regime of Marshal Pétain, Loire-Atlantique (and its capital Nantes) was separated from the rest of Brittany. Recovering the Loire-Atlantique has been a rallying cry of the Breton political movement ever since 1941. Our poll suggests strong public support for the reunification of historic Brittany (61 per cent). This attachment to the physical embodiment of historic Brittany is itself a powerful form of 'regionality effect'. Our survey demonstrates that it is shared across the political and geographical spectrum, with only minor variations according to *département*, partisan allegiance or other variables.

In Wales, the poll was primarily designed to measure general attitudes towards devolution in Wales and the National Assembly during the first two years of its operation. By any measure the National Assembly's formative years have been stormy. The wafer-thin majority in the 1997 referendum raised doubts about the commitment of the Welsh voters and the legitimacy of the whole project. The departure of one Welsh secretary (Ron Davies), and the appointment of another (Alun Michael) generally regarded as having been imposed by Tony Blair did little to enhance the devolutionary process. Furthermore, the failure of the Welsh Labour Party to win an overall majority in the first Assembly elections frustrated the expectation of strong and consistent policies, arguably one of the main justifications for devolution. The resultant scenario of 'all-party inclusive policy-making' was less than convincing and eventually led to Alun Michael's losing a vote of no confidence. It was against this background of institutional initiatives, political experimentation and plain damage limitation that our poll of Welsh public opinion was taken in late June 2001.

The results presented in Table 11.1 are remarkable on three counts. Only 24 per cent supported the pre-devolution arrangements. The prediction by Ron Davies that devolution would be a process rather than an event appeared to have been vindicated. Furthermore, 49 per cent of respondents supported the strengthening of the National Assembly to give it powers at least equivalent to those of the Scottish Parliament. This shift in public opinion is consistent with the majority view encountered in over forty interviews in and around the National Assembly that the current system suffers from a lack of clarity and a confused and unworkable attribution of functions. Our in-depth interviews demonstrated a deep-seated dissatisfaction with the devolution introduced by the Government of Wales Act and a desire to move towards primary legislative powers. The Welsh, while never the constitutional pace-setters, now look to follow Scotland's lead.

Other findings from the poll confirmed the Welsh public's more positive attitude to the devolution process in Wales. When asked the question, 'What are your personal views on devolution for Wales, that is the creation of the National Assembly for Wales, which has taken over responsibility for areas such as health and education in Wales?', a majority (51 per cent) were in favour or strongly in favour of devolution, with only 32 per cent against.[5] There would appear to have been a shift in popular opinion since the Welsh referendum in 1997. When asked more specific questions about the effectiveness of the National Assembly, the Welsh people appeared to be less confident about the Assembly. Firstly, the majority (60 per cent) of those asked disagreed with the statement that 'The quality of public services has improved under the Assembly', indicating that the Welsh public is still waiting for 'the Assembly to deliver'. This is to be expected. The Assembly was only two years old during the polling exercise and only in the longer term will it be able to impact on the deep-seated economic and social problems facing the country. On the issue of whether the existence of the Assembly has democratized political processes in Wales, respondents were split almost evenly, with a small majority against the proposition that 'The say of people in decision-making has improved under the Assembly'. This is an immediate problem for the Assembly which appears to reflect the general disillusionment with politics in the UK, indicated by the low general election turnout of 2001. The Assembly still needs to convince a large section of the Welsh public that devolution is bringing Welsh politics closer to the Welsh people. Proponents of devolution and the Welsh Assembly Government in particular will take comfort from the slight majority of people who agreed that 'The existence of the Assembly has given Wales more lobbying power within the UK government'. This view represents a quite sophisticated assessment, recognizing, on the one hand, the limited nature of the legislative powers devolved to Wales and, on the other, the enhanced lobbying capacity exercised by a 'democratic Assembly' compared with a secretary of state heading a small central-government department. We draw the conclusion, as in the *Western Mail* leader, that public opinion is 'warming to the Assembly'.

We deduce a strong underpinning of support for regional political institutions in Wales and Brittany. But these basic similarities mask essential differences between Wales and Brittany. This becomes apparent when we consider preferences for regional expenditure.

WHAT PRIORITIES FOR REGIONAL ACTION?

Regional public spending priorities are indicative not only of actual policy choices, but also of the appropriateness of public intervention of different levels in specific policy fields. Even in the most federally inclined system, it would be difficult to imagine defence expenditure being a major priority for a sub-central authority. The survey proceeded to ask an open-ended question ('If your region had more money to spend, where should its first two priorities lie?') seeking to elicit the Welsh and Breton public's preferences for regional public expenditure. Table 11.2 presents a hierarchy of the first preferences. We now consider the implications of these figures for Wales and Brittany.

TABLE **11.2**
First priority for regional expenditure in Wales and Brittany

Breton first priority	%	Welsh first priority	%
Environmental issues	20	NHS/hospitals	43
Economic development	9	Schools/education	21
Improving the roads	9	Public transport	6
Tourism	8	Getting people into jobs	4
Training	6	Urban development	3
Culture	5	Improving the roads	3
Education	5	Support for small business	2
Urban development	4	Environmental issues	2
Rural assistance	3	Children's facilities	2
Public transport	3	Other	5
Sport	2	Don't know/nothing	9
Other	15		
Don't know/nothing	11		

Public opinion in Wales has fully integrated the significance of devolution into its thinking. Its priorities for future regional expenditure involve generic spending areas – such as health and education – rather than more narrowly defined Welsh interests such as culture or language. The priorities for Assembly expenditure are broadly in line with those of the UK as a whole. Health and education are the overwhelming concerns, with the Welsh electorate demonstrating an awareness that the Assembly now makes many essential decisions in these areas. Health and education are two areas where the Assembly has devolved powers to define and apply Welsh solutions. The lessons for the Assembly are mixed. On the one hand, the salience of these issue areas justifies the search for Welsh solutions to intractable policy problems (of educational underachievement or of health standards below the UK average).[6] On the other hand, not only do health and education present seemingly irresolvable policy dilemmas, but both fields also contain their own complex pre-existing actor systems and their own path dependencies. Health and education symbolize the semi-sovereign nature of Assembly policy-making. There is a gulf between the expectations placed on the Assembly and the constraints of interdependent, semi-sovereign politics (Cole and Storer, 2002). There is no general legislative competency for the Assembly in these devolved areas: the Assembly can only act where it has a statutory basis for action. It can decide to shift resources to health or education, but some other policy field will lose out. As 'Treasury rules' apply to Wales, the Treasury continues to control the purse strings. Without tax-varying powers, the Assembly depends upon executive-led negotiations with the Treasury, which are undertaken by the secretary of state and not by the Assembly itself (which must, however, be consulted).

That the Assembly makes a difference is not in doubt, however. Its existence has proved a powerful bargaining chip with the Treasury, testified by the resources obtained in the last two budgetary rounds. The Assembly can engage many reforms which are resource neutral: the power of the purse does not determine everything. Its impact can be demonstrated in the sphere of education and lifelong learning, one of our fields of investigation. It has abolished the Training and Enterprise Councils (TECs) and created a complex new institutional structure co-ordinated by Education and Learning Wales (ELWa). In the field of pre-16 education, it has rejected premier Blair's specialist schools and pledged to retain the comprehensive system. It has also rejected all private finance initiatives in education. But education is an area of interdependent policy-making and the Assembly does not exercise control over all secondary legislation concerning education in Wales. One interviewee lamented the fact that 'since devolution, more secondary legislation affecting Wales on education has been passed through the Westminster parliament than the Assembly'. Teacher's pay and conditions in particular were entirely decided by London. In the area of health, the Assembly has reformed the structures of health care (the creation of area-wide NHS offices) and enacted a number of symbolic egalitarian measures (such as free eye tests for pensioners), but the specific solutions it can adopt are limited within the structures of the NHS as it currently exists.

The counterpart to the Welsh electorate's concern with health and education is that other Assembly priorities – such as the environment, social inclusion, transport, urban development and rural assistance – did not figure highly in the public's perceptions of important spending priorities. This hierarchy confirms the polity-building dimension of Welsh devolution that we explore below. While polity-building is deeply satisfying, there is a danger that the Assembly (and the Welsh Assembly Government in particular) will be identified in the eyes of public opinion as a rather distant Cardiff-based administration rather than a proximate authority bringing decision-making closer to the people.

In Brittany, the findings differ in important respects from those observed in Wales, where health and education dominated popular preferences. These results do not imply that the Breton public cares less about health and education. In the Breton case, expenditure priorities demonstrated a realistic appraisal of the limited powers of the French regions much more than a lack of interest in the areas of health and education. Breton public opinion has fully integrated the constraints of decentralization into its preferences. It is because health and education are not identified as areas of regional policy intervention that they do not appear as high priorities for regional expenditure. We would certainly not expect health to top the list of spending priorities for a French regional assembly. The French system of health care is elaborately – and expensively – managed by a social partnership of employers and trade unions, increasingly closely monitored by the central state. The regions do not have any responsibilities therein (though the *départements* do). The low ranking of education is rather more intriguing. Though France prides itself on its national education system, implying uniform standards and practices throughout the country, French regions also have important responsibilities in secondary and higher education. The regions build and maintain upper secondary schools (*lycées*) and some universities, provide equipment, participate in educational planning and – of great importance in Brittany – can make grants to private schools. Education is by far the largest spending post of all French regions, around 50 per cent in the case of Brittany. We surmise that, though there is intense interest in Brittany in education, this issue area is perceived primarily either as a national or a more localized policy responsibility. The regional councils have not yet drawn much political capital from their major budgetary investment in education over the past fifteen years. Education is one area where the central state has succeeded in shedding responsibilities to the periphery (regional councils and state field services) while retaining strategic control (Balme, 1999).

Unlike in Wales, in the case of Brittany the public's expenditure preferences pinpoint issues of specific regional importance, rather than generic spending areas. They suggest a strong 'regional effect'. The first priority was the environment. Environmental issues are high on the political agenda in Brittany, which has to face specific challenges unknown to most other French regions. The second priority for regional expenditure identified in the survey is economic development. There is an established post-war tradition of public intervention in supporting the Breton economy, whether through direct investment or through providing transport infrastructure. By distinguishing economic development as the second priority for regional expenditure, the Breton public again identified an area where regional action could (or should) make a difference. Amongst the other priorities for regional expenditure we can identify two further areas closely linked to the specific attributes of Brittany: tourism and culture. Brittany is one of France's major tourist regions. That Bretons look to the regional authority to promote tourism supports the proximity argument; regional investment is appropriate because the region has detailed knowledge of local conditions. We might make a similar observation with respect to culture. It is entirely appropriate for the regional authority to promote culture, not only because culture is worth promoting, but also because it has a strong regional dimension.

In Wales and Brittany, we subjected two policy areas to more intense scrutiny: training and regional languages. In Brittany, as in Wales, support for expenditure on regional languages was very low down the list of popular priorities – fewer than 1 per cent of first preferences in both cases. We should exercise some caution when interpreting this figure. Priorities for public expenditure do not automatically equate with issue saliency. In an area such as support for regional languages, policy objectives might be achieved with minimal additional public expenditure. In Wales (50 per cent) and in Brittany (53 per cent) a majority of respondents identified the National Assembly for Wales or the Brittany regional council as the appropriate level for decision-making on language-related issues. The findings for training policy provide further support for the regional level in both countries. Welsh and Breton public opinion was remarkably similar in preferring the regional institution as the 'primary political institution making decisions in the area of training policy', rather than the EU, national government or local government.[7]

Our second series of questions lead us to refine our argument somewhat. A logic of appropriateness appears to be at work. Whether consciously or not, the Welsh public appears to have integrated the evolutionary character of devolution into its calculations. It looks to the Assembly (in an exaggerated manner) to concentrate its resources on remedying deep-rooted problems in health and education. To all extents and purposes, the Welsh public implores its Assembly to act as a government, divided opinions over devolution notwithstanding. The Breton public wants regional public expenditure to be concentrated in areas where regional institutions might make a difference, or where the image of Brittany itself is involved. We might conceive of this as a bounded regionality. There is no equivalent process of state-building to that one might infer from the findings in Wales. Health and education provide a useful contrast to training and regional languages. In the core areas of health and education, even in regionally minded Brittany, there is a preference for a system of national regulation, consistent with French public service doctrine, equality of standards and the legacy of 150 years of 'republican' ideology.

INSTITUTIONS, IDENTITIES AND VOTING INTENTIONS IN WALES AND BRITTANY

How best can we comprehend these institutional viewpoints in Wales and Brittany? Full analysis of the structural and attitudinal variables contained in the poll lies outside the scope of the present article. We will limit our analysis here to two criteria – multiple identities and intended voting behaviour in an Assembly or regional election – which allow for meaningful comparisons to be drawn between Welsh and Breton public opinion.

Does identity matter? We asked respondents in both surveys to state whether they considered themselves to be more Welsh than British (more Breton than French), equally Welsh and British (equally Breton and French) or more British than Welsh (more French than Breton). The results are presented in Table 11.3. The table is highly revealing. A far higher proportion of the Welsh survey – around one-third – considered itself to be exclusively or primarily Welsh than was the case in Brittany. A sense of Welshness as being essentially opposed to Britishness is firmly rooted in a sizeable minority of Welsh people. In Brittany, by contrast, the sense of regional identity is strong, but this is not considered as being in opposition to an overarching French nationhood. Regional identity is not a surrogate nationality. This finding is consistent with the mainstream portrayal of Breton political culture and society we investigated above. There is much less of a conflict between Breton and French identities than is the case for Wales and the UK. The greatest difference between Wales and Brittany, therefore, lies not so much in institutional preferences for the future as in the linkage

TABLE **11.3**

The Moreno identity scale for Brittany and Wales

Brittany	%	Commentary	Wales	%
Breton, not French More Breton than French	17	The results of centuries of 'national' assimilation is to suppress a homogeneous Breton identity; regional identity remains strong	Welsh, not British More Welsh than British	37
Equally Breton and French	56	Confirms representation of the legitimist nature of Breton political culture	Equally Welsh and British	35
More French than Breton French, not Breton	26	Three-quarters express some sort of Breton identity, in spite of traditions of Jacobin centralization	More British than Welsh British, not Welsh	22
Don't know	1			
Other				6

between national and regional identities. Multiple identities are more easily assumed in Brittany than in Wales.

Simple cross-tabulations suggest that in the two cases there is some sort of relationship between identity and institutional preferences. Clear relationships were established between identity and institutional preferences at the two extremes. Those considering themselves to be uniquely or predominantly Welsh or Breton were far more likely to advocate either a Scottish-style parliament or independence (autonomy in the case of Brittany) than were those considering themselves to be primarily or entirely British or French. There also appears to be some sort of relationship between the ability to speak a regional language (Breton or Welsh) and an institutional preference in favour of greater regionalization or autonomy. Our poll suggests that fluency in the Welsh language appears to be a major explanatory factor of institutional preferences. Those declaring themselves to be fluent in Welsh (some 12 per cent) were more likely to espouse an independent Wales than those with little or no knowledge of the language. A similar finding was observed in Brittany, though the numbers were smaller.

Do partisan preferences matter? We asked both populations how they intended to vote if a general or a regional election were to be held tomorrow. We then cross-tabulated regional voting intention with institutional

TABLE 11.4

Institutional preferences and multiple identities in Wales (% rounded up or down)

	Welsh, not British	More Welsh than British	Equally Welsh and British	More British than Welsh
Wales should become independent	26	18	4	4
Remain part of the UK, with elected parliament	41	44.5	39	30
Remain part of the UK, with elected assembly	15	24	26	25
Remain part of the UK without an elected assembly	13	12	30	36

TABLE 11.5

Institutional preferences and multiple identities in Brittany (% rounded up or down)

	Breton but not French	More Breton than French	Equally Breton and French	More French than Breton	French but not Breton
Abolish the *Conseil Regional*	–	1	2	2	1
The *Conseil Regional* should remain with limited powers	29	31.5	42	57.5	56
Give the *Conseil Regional* law-making and taxation powers	19	35	36	33	20
Brittany should become independent	33	25	10	3	15

preferences (and, in the case of Brittany, with attitudes towards recovering the Loire-Atlantique). In Brittany, we observed surprisingly few differences according to voting intention. Socialist Party (PS) voters were scarcely more favourable than RPR voters to enhanced regional autonomy. Though we must treat these figures with caution, they bear out the belief expressed in many interviews that institutional preferences cut across existing parties. Institutional choices can not be reduced to a simple left–right cleavage. The RPR president of the Brittany region, Josselin de Rohan, might have a sceptical position on greater autonomy, but many RPR voters did not share this view. Likewise, while the Socialist Party leader Jean-Yves Le Drian has repositioned the party in favour of greater regional autonomy, more socialist voters are happy with existing arrangements than in favour of a Scottish-style parliament. These findings are consistent with existing representations of Breton political cleavages. There is a moderation of

TABLE 11.6
Voting intention in a National Assembly for Wales election and institutional preference (% rounded up or down)

	Con	Lab	Lib Dem	Plaid Cymru	Total
An independent Wales	4.5	7	1	28	11
Remain part of the UK, with elected parliament	24	44	43	51	38
Remain part of the UK, with elected assembly	17	30	27	12	23
Remain part of the UK without an elected assembly	54	15	27	6	23.5
Don't know	–	3.6	1.4	2.3	4.1

TABLE 11.7
Voting intention in a Brittany Regional election and institutional preference (% rounded up or down)

	Total	PS	Greens	RPR	UDF
Regional council with limited powers	44	49	45.5	54	42
Elected parliament with tax-raising and legislative powers	34	36	39	32	46
Autonomy for Brittany	12	8	14	6	4
Strongly in favour and in favour of uniting Loire-Atlantique département with Brittany	63	67	68	62	79

political conflict within the Brittany arena. Moreover, national political parties are infused with Breton cultural values. There is also a distrust of political extremes, except in specific sub-cultural circumstances. While not going as far as to suggest a cross-partisan consensus on the broad issues facing Brittany, there is an underlying consensus to defend Breton interests to the outside world and limit political conflict.

Such a consensus is less obviously apparent in the case of Wales. Within the Welsh electorate, we can identity three distinct positions, ranging from a residual Conservative hostility to the principle of devolution, to overwhelming support from intending Plaid voters for at least a Scottish-style parliament, with Labour and Liberal Democrats occupying a median position favourable to going beyond executive devolution. Rather like the

AMs interviewed, few support the existing settlement, with the status quo option arriving in third position in each electorate ('retain an elected Assembly with limited powers'). Executive devolution appears as the hollow core of regional governance in Wales.

Our findings are nonetheless remarkable. Only the Conservative section of the electorate continues to oppose devolution, by a small margin. Devolution is a cleavage that has traditionally cut across existing political parties, most especially the Labour Party. The principle of an elected Assembly/ Parliament is now accepted overwhelmingly in each section of the electorate, except that of the Conservatives. While divisions remain in each party, the centre of gravity amongst intending Labour and Liberal Democrat voters (the governing coalition) has shifted beyond accepting devolution towards advocating a Scottish-style parliament. The Plaid Cymru section of the electorate is the most cohesive, in its large majority dissatisfied with the limited devolution introduced by the Government of Wales Act.

We can observe this paradigm shift in favour of devolution in operation at the level of political practice and inter-party relations. The founding fathers were convinced that the majoritarian traditions of Westminster politics would be inappropriate for Wales. The rhetorical commitment to all-inclusive politics implied new forms of cross-party dialogue and the involvement of non-governing parties in policy-making decisions. The arrival in power of Rhodri Morgan and the creation of the Labour–Liberal Democrat coalition in September 2000 marked two important watersheds in the history of Welsh politics. The victory of Rhodri Morgan represented the coming of age of a specifically Welsh Labour Party, cognisant above all of its core territorial interests. Party opponents, even when critical of the coalition, recognize the emancipation of the Welsh Labour Party. The formation of the Lib–Lab coalition was difficult to square with 'all-inclusivity', especially as Rhodri Morgan does not conceal his preference for a single-party administration after the 2003 elections. In some important respects, however, all Welsh parties have moved closer together since 1999. There is general agreement across all parties that the Assembly's powers need to be revised, though institutional preferences differ greatly. For the UK-based parties, moreover, there is an awareness that devolution encourages a territorial adjustment of their core political message. Even the Welsh Conservatives have learned this lesson. In extensive interviews in and around the National Assembly in 2001 and 2002, Assembly members from all parties expressed strong demands for new powers. Deprived of full legislative powers in the transferred domains, the National Assembly lacks the legal and political means for its policy ambitions. Even the Conservative group accepted that a clarification of the Assembly's powers was essential; such a clarification will await the next election at the earliest.

In association with a narrowing of positions within and between parties, our findings also suggest that traditional regional cleavages have lessened in intensity. The gap between those regions most favourable and least favourable to devolution is only 9 per cent. There is little regional difference in the preferences for future political developments. The Scottish option, a parliament with law-making and taxation powers wins almost equal support across Wales, with the exception of Cardiff which is most sceptical of such a change. However, strongest support is expressed almost equally in north and south: 42 per cent in north-west Wales and 43 per cent in the Valleys. The figures suggest that a more cohesive Welsh attitude to devolution is emerging across the whole of Wales.

CONCLUSION

Devolution and decentralization in Wales and Brittany are best understood as two alternative forms of territorial institution-building. We observed above that, in important respects, the Wales–Brittany comparison is asymmetrical. There are certain disadvantages in asymmetrical comparisons, but there are also countervailing arguments. As developed throughout this article, devolution and decentralization present two alternative models: one focused on territorial identity and polity-building, the other on proximity as a response to policy solutions. Comparing comparable regions, even in distinctive institutional settings, allows for judgements to be made about the efficacy or otherwise of specific regional political institutions. A fuller comparison of devolution and decentralization in Wales and Brittany would need to go beyond measuring institutional preferences, the purpose of this article. We need to develop an index that combines criteria drawn from the study of institutions, networks, social capital, identity formation, public policy co-ordination and central regulation. Such an index would allow a more realistic appreciation of the potential for regional governance than a limited description of rule-making capacity.

While awaiting such an exercise, the present article has focused on comparing public opinion and political institutions in two neighbouring EU states. From our empirical investigations we observe rather different processes at work in Brittany and Wales. Devolution in Wales emerges as a dynamic process with unintended consequences. When evaluating the potential for regional governance in Wales, we must draw a distinction between constitutional constraint and political dynamic. Constitutionally, the power to act is spread across endless acts of Parliament. Politically, a consensus is emerging within Wales for a strengthening of the powers of the Assembly. This consensus represents a paradigm shift by comparison even with the results of the Welsh referendum in 1997. The question is no longer whether devolution will survive, but whether the Welsh Assembly should be given powers equivalent to those in Scotland. This consensus has solid support within public opinion.

No such conclusion can be drawn in Brittany where, in spite of a strong undercurrent of support for a federal evolution, the status quo is the most widely supported position. Taken as a whole, Breton public opinion adopts a median position. There is little appetite for autonomy. This can be gauged by several criteria: the weak level of support for autonomist parties; the lack of consistent positions one way or the other from the main parties; the real, but limited, constituency declaring itself in favour of autonomy; the Brittany-specific focus of regional expenditure priorities. Bretons are widely attached to a legitimist form of regionalism. There is a strong sense of regional distinctiveness, but also a deeply embedded reluctance to transgress the established order. On the other hand, our findings suggest on balance that, while respectful of established norms and processes, the Breton public would welcome a move towards greater regionalization. Almost one half (45 per cent) of the Breton public supported going beyond the existing limited form of French decentralization and adopting powers analogous to those of the Scottish Parliament.

Politicians in both regions refer to traditions, or ambitions of all-inclusivity. Evidence from our quantitative and qualitative investigations suggests a more comfortable and harmonious relationship between identity, institutions and territory in the case of Brittany than in Wales. There is a definite tension between being British and being Welsh for around one-third of Welsh people. The proportion of those constructing their Breton identity against being French is much weaker. Divisions within Breton society are less affirmed than in Wales, where linguistic, territorial and political divisions persist, in spite of a rallying to the new devolved institutions.

Wales has a more developed system of political devolution than Brittany, but in many other respects it can learn from observing the French region. Welsh politicians tend to engage in aspirational comparisons with Catalonia, Ireland or Canada, but these are quite unrealistic. Welsh politicians need to encourage something akin to the pride in being Breton:

that is, a non-exclusive identity broadly shared across the political spectrum and within Breton society. Wales needs to look to the example of regions such as Brittany which harness their identity to developing a strong sense of social and human capital.

NOTES

1. Research for this article was carried out as part of the ESRC's devolution and constitutional change programme ('Devolution and Decentralisation in Wales and Brittany': grant number L 219 25 2007). The award holders are Alistair Cole (principal researcher), Barry Jones, John Loughlin and Colin Williams. Alan Storer is the research assistant. The award is based in the school of European studies at Cardiff University (the department of Welsh is also involved). We thank the council for its support.

2. Market Research Wales and Efficience 3 simultaneously carried out the public opinion surveys in Wales and Brittany in June and July 2001. A representative sample of 1,007, selected by quotas of age, gender, socio-economic group and locality, was interviewed in each region.

3. These examples were those most frequently cited in extensive interviews in and around the National Assembly for Wales in 2001 and 2002. Interviews took place in the following organizations: the National Assembly for Wales, ELWa, the CCETs, business organizations (CBI, FSB, Chambers-Wales, IoD, House-Builders Federation, the Economic Fora), trade unions (TUC, GMB, Unify), WEFO, WDA, local government, WLB, New Deal Taskforce, CCW, European Commission, EOC. Interviews are ongoing. All interviewees were guaranteed anonymity.

4. Direct election is a slight misnomer. Up to and including 1998, elections for the French regional councils took place on the basis of departmental party lists. The proportional representation system used – a 5 per cent threshold and the 'highest average' methods of allocating votes to seats – marginally favoured the larger parties. The electoral constituency for the 2004 elections will probably be that of the region, rather than the *départements*.

5. The precise results were as follows: strongly in favour 11 per cent, in favour 40 per cent, against 19 per cent, strongly against 13 per cent, don't know 18 per cent.

6. The situation is, however, regionally differentiated. In relation to education, standards across Wales are very varied, with high levels in rural areas, but much lower ones in the declining industrial areas, especially in the Valleys. The pattern for health is rather similar. The Valleys are a health black spot, where the situation is compounded by the high rate of respiratory illnesses. As in Brittany, demands on healthcare are exacerbated by the high numbers of elderly pensioners retiring in Wales.

7. In the case of Brittany, 43.5 per cent favoured the regional council as the appropriate level for training policy, followed by 24.5 per cent for local government, 20.5 per cent for central government and only 3.1 per cent for the European Union. In the case of Wales the figures were the Assembly (41.5 per cent) the UK government (25.3 per cent), local government (23.4 per cent) and the European Union (3.1 per cent).

REFERENCES

Balme, R. (1999). *Les Politiques de Néo-régionalisme*, Paris, Economica.
Chaney, P., Hall, T. and Pithouse, A. (eds) (2001). *Post-Devolution Wales: New Governance – New Democracy?* Cardiff, University of Wales Press.
Cole, A. and John, P. (2001). *Local Governance in England and France*, London, Routledge.
Cole, A. and Storer, A. (2002). 'An emerging policy community', in Jones, J. B. and Osmond, J. (eds), *Creating a Civic Culture*, Cardiff, IWA.
Dupoirier, E. (ed.) (1998). *Régions, la Croisée des Chemins*, Paris, Presses de Sciences Po.
Favereau, F. (1993). *Bretagne Contemporaine: Langue, Culture, Identité*, Morlaix, Editions Skol Vreizh.
Flatres, P. (1986). *La Bretagne*, Paris, PUF.
Ford, C. (1993). *Creating the Nation in Provincial France: Religion and Political Identity in Brittany*, Princeton, Princeton University Press.
Jones, J. B. and Osmond, J. (eds) (2002). *Creating a Civic Culture*, Cardiff, IWA.
Le Bourdonnec, Y. (1996). *Le Miracle Breton*, Paris, Calmann-Lévy.
Le Coadic, R. (1998). *L'Identité Bretonne*, Rennes, Presses Universitaires de Rennes.
Loughlin, J. and Mazey, S. (eds) (1995). *The End of the French Unitary State: Ten Years of Regionalization in France, 1982–1992*, London, Frank Cass.
Marinetto, M. (2001). 'The new settlement and the process of devolution: territorial politics and governance under the Welsh Assembly', *Political Studies*, 49, 2, 306–22.
Martray, J. (1983). *Vingt ans qui transformèrent la Bretagne. L'epopée du CELIB*, Paris, France Empire.
McAllister, L. (2000). 'The new politics in Wales: rhetoric or reality?', *Parliamentary Affairs*, 53, 3, 591–604.
Nay, O. (1997). *La Région, une Institution. La Représentation, le Pouvoir et la Règle dans l'Espace Régional*, Paris, l'Harmattan.
Patchett, K. (2000). 'The New Welsh Constitution: The Government of Wales Act 1998', in Barry Jones and Denis Balsom (eds.), *The Road to the National Assembly for Wales*, Cardiff: University of Wales Press, p. 229.
Pillet, D. (2001). 'La Bretagne. Un modèle? Non, un exemple', *Ouest-France*, 23 November.
Rawlings, R. (1998). 'The new model Wales', *Journal of Law and Society* 25, 4, 461–509.
Rawlings, R. (2001). 'Quasi-legislative devolution: powers and principles', unpublished paper considered by the National Assembly Review Procedure.

12. THE WELSH ECONOMY: A STATISTICAL PROFILE

David Brooksbank

INTRODUCTION

This article is the annual statistical profile of the Welsh economy. The format in terms of statistical content remains the same as that which appears in volumes 9 to 14 inclusive of *Contemporary Wales*. The discussion in the main text covers seven topics: Output, Income and Expenditure; Employment; Unemployment; Earnings; House Prices and Regional Competitiveness. The sixteen tables are based on information made available prior to 1 June 2002 and, as noted in previous surveys, compilation and production lags with respect to certain official statistics mean that 'latest' figures occasionally 'lag' by two or three years.

Much of the focus of this edition of *Contemporary Wales* is on the slowly emerging impact that the European Structural Funds are having on both the economy and society of the country. The first rounds of expenditure under the European Structural Fund arrangements have now been underway for approximately eighteen months and many of the initial 'fast track' projects are nearing the stage of completion or extension. The first chance to evaluate the programmes and change the way in which the Single Programming Documents target particular development needs will come at the end of 2002. As noted in *Contemporary Wales* for the past four years, the information summarized in the tables below illustrates the profound nature of the economic development challenges that still lie ahead. Under the guidance of a new administration, commentators and analysts alike await the publication of each new set of economic data with keen anticipation. The unprecedented scrutiny which economic development initiatives and programmes will undergo during this period of European funding has concentrated the minds of policy-makers on securing real change and improvement. The recent formation of another quango, the Economic Advisory Board, reporting directly to the First Minister on the progress of particular phases of economic development activity gives a clue as to the importance attached to this area by the coalition administration. The publication of the economic strategy, *A Winning Wales* (NAW, 2001), was roundly criticized by many in the media as unachievable and it will be interesting to chart the progress of the economy against the ambitious targets for growth over the coming decade. Indeed, it is the role of independent commentaries such as this to report on the impact of regeneration strategies as they effect the underlying macro-economic statistics. In this review appropriate data is available at a Unitary Authority (UA) level; where comparisons are made with other UK regions, the article refers to Government Office Regions.

OUTPUT, INCOME AND EXPENDITURE

Gross Domestic Product (GDP) remains the most widely used indicator of economic activity and is the most commonly used means of comparing both national and regional performance. Table 12.1 gives details of the GDP per head at factor cost figures for the Government Office Regions of the UK in 1999. These are the latest 'provisional' figures available at the time of writing and show that GDP per head in Wales was £10,400, an increase of 5.2 per cent over the figure for 1998. This meant that in 1999 Wales had a GDP per head of 80.5 per cent of the UK average, maintaining its relative position above Northern Ireland and the North East, but locked firmly in the lowest group of regions.

These provisional figures remain the same as those reported in last year's commentary. They show that annual growth for the UK (excluding the Extra-Regio figures which include UK workers in embassies abroad and UK armed services stationed abroad) was 3.8 per cent in 1999. The South East had the highest growth at 5.1 per cent. Annual growth was lowest in the North East at 2.3 per cent. GDP per head in London (£16,900) was 30 per cent higher than the UK average of £13,000. In Northern Ireland and the North East it was 23 per cent lower.

Table 12.1 also shows figures for Household Disposable Income per head. In 1999 Wales had household disposable income per head of £9,113, with only Northern Ireland and the North East having a lower level. This represents 90.4 per cent of the UK average, which stands at £10,088. The table also shows individual consumption expenditure per head. In 1999

TABLE **12.1**
Regional accounts, 1999

	GDP per head at basic prices		Household disposable income per head		Individual consumption expenditure per head	
	£	% of UK	£	% of UK	£	% of UK
London	16900	130.0	12036	119.4	12250	124.2
South East	15100	116.4	11249	111.6	11392	115.5
East	15100	116.2	11255	111.7	10077	102.2
South West	11800	90.8	9825	97.5	9600	97.3
West Midlands	11900	91.7	9195	91.2	9262	93.9
East Midlands	12100	93.6	9346	92.7	9057	91.8
Yorkshire & the Humber	11400	87.9	9305	92.3	8907	90.3
North West	11300	86.9	9375	93.0	9321	94.5
North East	10000	77.3	8353	82.9	8003	81.1
England	13300	102.4	10237	101.6	10057	102.0
Scotland	12500	96.5	9558	94.8	9459	95.9
Northern Ireland	10100	77.5	8659	85.9	8281	83.9
WALES	10400	80.5	9113	90.4	8206	83.2
UNITED KINGDOM	13000	100	10088	100	9864	100

Note 1: Figures are consistent with the 2000 UK National Accounts – provisional figures.
Note 2: The differences between the old Standard Statistical Regions (SSRs) and the Government Office Regions (GORs) are that East Anglia SSR is combined with Essex, Hertfordshire and Bedfordshire to create the new Eastern GOR; London is a separate GOR; and Cumbria transfers from the old North SSR to the new North West GOR with the remainder of the North SSR becoming the North East GOR.
Note 3: Based on the European System of Accounts 1995 (ESA95).

Source: Office for National Statistics.

Wales had a figure of £8,206, with only the North East having a lower level of expenditure. This represents a gap of 16.8 percentage points below the UK average and is symptomatic of a low-wage economy.

There continues to be substantial diversity between the regions of the UK. Scotland, Wales, Northern Ireland and the regions of England are all different in character, industrial structure and economic performance. Scotland, for example, has the largest area, but has a small population relative to its size; London has by far the smallest area, but the second largest population (after the South East) – over 7 million. In 1999 Wales had 5 per cent of the population, 4.5 per cent of the total of economically active persons, 3.9 per cent of the UK's GDP, 4.3 per cent of individual consumption expenditure and only 4.2 per cent of household income.

TABLE 12.2

Index of production and construction for Wales, (a) seasonally adjusted, (b) 1995 = 100

| 1992 STANDARD INDUSTRIAL CLASSIFICATION | | | 1995 weights per thousand | Annual Indices | | Quarterly Indices | | | | | Percentage change over latest 4 quarters on | |
Section	Sub-Section	Description		2000	2001	2000 Qtr 4	2001 Qtr1	2001 Qtr21	2001 Qtr3	2001 Qtr4	WALES	UK
C–F		Production and construction	1000	100.3	93.2	98.7	96.0	91.4	92.8	92.4	−7.1	−1.4
C–E		Production industries	860	102.6	95.1	101.5	98.1	93.9	94.5	93.9	−7.3	−2.2
C		Mining and quarrying	26	66.7	63.4	67.9	65.3	65.0	61.7	61.7	−5.0	−4.9
D		Manufacturing (revised definition)	752	105.4	96.7	104.6	100.5	97.2	94.9	94.1	−8.3	−2.3
	DA	Food products, beverages and tobacco	77	108	102	106	106	102	99	102	−5.5	1.4
	DB–DC	Textiles, textile products, leather and leather products	21	81	62	72	68	64	60	58	−22.6	−12.1
	DE	Pulp, paper and paper products: printing and publishing	59	92	98	94	96	96	100	98	5.9	−1.8
	DF	Coke and refined petroleum products	14	91	83	93	76	81	87	89	−8.9	−2.9
	DG	Chemicals, chemical products and man-made fibres	82	102	101	103	101	101	100	100	−1.5	3.9
	DI	Other non-metallic mineral products	22	86	89	85	85	88	91	91	2.7	0.9
	DJ	Basic metals and fabricated metal products	193	99	85	99	90	88	83	79	−14.5	−3.1
	DK	Machinery and equipment not elsewhere classified	38	101	98	105	107	97	93	95	−2.8	0.8
	DL	Electrical and optical equipment	106	132	107	133	116	110	102	101	−18.9	−8.0
	DM	Transport equipment	67	126	127	122	133	126	126	125	1.2	−2.8
	DD, DH, DN	Other manufacturing (inc. rubber, plastic & wood)	74	92	87	89	87	84	85	89	−6.3	n/a
E		Electricity, gas and water supply	82	88.0	90.7	84.2	86.1	73.4	101.5	102.0	3.1	1.0
F		Construction	140	86.3	81.3	81.3	83.4	76.1	82.4	83.4	−5.8	3.1

Notes: a – Revisions to the series are normally made each quarter to take account both of more recent information and improved seasonal factors.
b – All series are seasonally adjusted unless otherwise stated in the note.

Source: Welsh Office.

TABLE 12.3
Identifiable general government expenditure: 2000–2001

	£ per head					Index (United Kingdom identifiable expenditure = 100)			
	England	Scotland	Wales	Northern Ireland	United Kingdom	England	Scotland	Wales	Northern Ireland
Agriculture, Fisheries, Food and Forestry	66	216	103	249	86	77	251	120	290
Trade, Industry, Energy and Employment	110	196	137	399	127	87	154	108	315
Roads and Transport	148	185	151	135	151	98	123	100	90
Housing	48	92	79	136	56	86	164	142	243
Other Environmental Services	151	200	258	165	161	94	124	160	103
Law, Order and Protective Services	326	353	314	723	339	96	104	93	213
Education	719	928	733	1033	747	96	124	98	138
Culture, Media and Sport	90	84	150	84	93	98	91	162	91
Health and Personal Social Services	1132	1347	1303	1283	1163	97	116	112	110
Social Security	1692	1920	2013	2077	1738	97	110	116	120
Miscellaneous[1]	47	38	59	139	50				
TOTAL	4529	5558	5302	6424	4709	96	118	113	136

Note: [1] Expenditure includes the costs of central administration of the offices of the Secretaries of State of the territorial departments.

Source: HM Treasury.

The wide variation in the size of the regions makes it difficult to compare the regions' economic performance using aggregate monetary totals; comparisons are therefore usually expressed in terms of amounts per head of the population. However, it is important to note that the growth in totals may be quite different to the growth per head in regions where the population has increased or decreased. Furthermore, the level per head is determined both by the average amount of 'cash' of the working population and by the proportion of dependents. In Northern Ireland, for example, households have a high proportion of children (24 per cent of the population were aged under sixteen in 1999 compared with 19 to 21 per cent in other regions). This will tend to depress amounts per head. Ideally, therefore, the age structure of the population should be taken into account when comparing figures on a per head basis.

Table 12.2 shows the index of production and construction for Wales. These figures are the same as last reported in *Contemporary Wales*, including as they do figures up to the third quarter of 2000. All figures relate to an index starting in 1995 and the 'other manufacturing' now includes wood products as well as rubber and plastic. As reported last year, despite pessimistic predictions, production industries and manufacturing rose by 2.4 and 3.5 per cent respectively over the previous year. Output in mining and quarrying continued to fall and saw a drop of 11.3 per cent in the same period. The index, relative to its 1995 level, fell further to 26, recognizing long-term decline in the primary production sector of the Welsh economy.

The manufacturing sector as a whole saw growth of 3.5 per cent over the last year. Breaking this total down into the relevant sectors, the largest falls were in the textiles (5.2 per cent) and pulp and paper products (3.9 per cent) categories. The fall in textiles reflects high-profile closures in Mid and West Wales following the decision by Marks and Spencer to source a larger proportion of its clothing products abroad. Substantial positive growth was seen in the electrical and optical equipment (12.7 per cent), basic metal fabrication (4.6 per cent) and transport equipment (3.2 per cent). Construction fell by 8.7 per cent in the 2000 figures following a number of years of steady growth.

A number of recent events are likely to influence these figures over the next few years as the economy adjusts. These include the announcement of job losses by steel makers Corus, which has announced job losses at its plants at Ebbw Vale, Shotton and Gorseinon, as well as a scaling down of production at Llanwern in Newport. There have also been further job losses in the textile industry in the Swansea and West Wales areas.

Table 12.3 shows identifiable government expenditure per head for the financial year 2000/1. These figures show that Wales, with a figure of £5,302, was the lowest of the three Celtic regions. The activities that grew most over that year, relative to the average UK expenditure per head, were agriculture, fisheries, food and forestry and culture, media and sport. The main area that shows a substantial decline in expenditure per head in Wales is housing. Interestingly this was one of the main areas emphasized for expansion by the incoming Labour Assembly government two years ago and it may be one area that has suffered in terms of budget as other areas have been given higher priority.

EMPLOYMENT

Tables 12.4 and 12.5 give information from the Labour Force Survey (LFS) about the workforce in Great Britain. Table 12.4 shows the seasonally adjusted figures for employees in employment by Government Office Region. Table 12.5 shows the sectoral breakdown by industry for Wales and Great Britain. The most recent data for these tables comes from the December 2001 to February 2002 quarterly LFS.

Table 12.4 shows that the employment rate across the UK has remained relatively stable over the past year. This has been reflected in a healthy and vibrant economy where consumer expenditure has remained buoyant and the fear of recession has not been widespread. As the figures for house prices and unemployment indicate later in this review, there has been a general feeling of optimism about the future, despite the potentially catastrophic impact of the terrorist attacks on 11 September. The LFS estimate of employment in Wales was 68.9 per cent in the December 2001–February 2002 period, very slightly down on the figure of 69.2 per cent for September–November 2000.

The table also shows that, whilst in Great Britain some 1.2 million jobs were created, only 46,000 of these were created in Wales. This represents only 3.8 per cent of new jobs, which is less than one would have predicted for Wales on a population basis. Looking at changes in employment by gender over the period shows that male employment fell by 0.2 percentage points nationally whilst in Wales it rose by 0.8 percentage points, equivalent to some 22,000 employees. Female employment remained static at 69.6 per cent nationally, whereas female employment in Wales rose by some 24,000 employees, despite a small fall in the rate of 1.2 percentage points. This phenomenon is likely to be a statistical anomaly that further corrections to the LFS employee data series next year will reverse.

TABLE 12.4

Employment: Wales, Great Britain and regions, Labour Force Survey employment, thousands, seasonally adjusted

	September–November 2000						December 2001–February 2002					
	Male	Rate (%)[2]	Female	Rate (%)[2]	Total	Rate (%)[2]	Male	Rate (%)[2]	Female	Rate (%)[2]	Total	Rate (%)[2]
London	1873	77.1	1428	63.9	3302	70.8	1995	76.8	1549	63.8	3544	70.6
South East	2208	85.6	1750	74.4	3958	80.3	2303	85.7	1876	74.4	4179	80.3
East	1471	84.7	1169	74.2	2640	79.7	1537	85.3	1240	73.3	2777	79.6
South West	1289	83.8	1042	74.8	2332	79.5	1326	82.6	1136	75.2	2462	79.1
West Midlands	1340	78.2	1042	68.1	2382	73.5	1393	79.5	1100	68.9	2492	74.5
East Midlands	1106	81.6	857	70.1	1963	76.2	1132	81.1	912	71.1	2043	76.3
Yorkshire & the Humber	1272	78.0	1019	70.1	2291	74.3	1314	78.7	1033	67.8	2347	73.6
North West	1685	76.7	1335	67.3	3020	72.2	1718	76.3	1424	68.3	3141	72.5
North East	604	73.5	479	63.9	1083	68.9	593	71.6	505	65.2	1099	68.6
Scotland	1270	77.6	1074	70.4	2344	74.1	1253	75.4	1118	70.3	2371	73.0
WALES	677	73.3	535	64.4	1212	69.2	699	74.1	559	63.2	1258	68.9
GREAT BRITAIN	14796	79.7	11731	69.6	26527	74.9	15263	79.5	12450	69.6	27713	74.8

Notes 1. Government Office Regions as described for Table 12.1.
    2. denominator is all persons of working age.

Source: Labour Market Trends, various issues.

TABLE 12.5

Employee jobs ('000s) in Great Britain and Wales, by industry (SIC92), December 2000 and December 2001

	Great Britain			Wales		
	Dec 2000	Dec 2001	*% change*	Dec 2000	Dec 2001	*% change*
Agriculture, hunting, forestry and fishing (A, B)	264	237	–10.2	16	13	–18.8
Mining & quarrying (C)	72	74	2.8	4	3	–25
Manufacturing (D)	3800	3646	–4.1	201	189	–6.0
Electricity, gas and water supply (E)	101	100	–1.0	5	4	–20
Construction (F)	1127	1210	7.4	57	57	0
Wholesale, retail, trade and repairs (G)	4405	4480	1.7	174	176	1.1
Hotels and restaurants (H)	1606	1613	0.4	67	66	–1.5
Transport, storage and communication (I)	1525	1520	–0.3	45	43	–4.4
Financial intermediation (J)	1065	1067	0.2	31	36	16.1
Real estate, renting and business activities (K)	3837	3856	–0.8	100	100	0
Public administration and defence: compulsory social security (L)	1344	1367	1.7	76	74	–2.6
Education (M)	2070	2108	1.8	104	107	2.9
Health and social work (N)	2652	2695	1.6	145	153	5.5
Other community, social and personal activities (O–Q)	1260	1259	0	57	56	–1.8
Service industries (G–Q)	19805	19932	0.6	799	811	1.5
Total male	12805	12589	–1.7	538	504	–6.3
Male part-time	1721	1752	1.8	72	78	8.3
Total female	12355	12641	2.3	543	574	5.7
Female part-time	5854	6179	5.0	275	308	12
TOTAL	25161	25230	0.3	1081	1077	–0.4

Note: Not seasonally adjusted.
Source: Labour Market Trends.

Table 12.5 shows the industry classification of employees in Great Britain and Wales. Again the dates reported have changed this year, with December 2001 figures being the most recent update. Here the data is derived from the Annual Employment Survey (AES) and shows that in the period December 2000 to December 2001, according to the AES, total employment fell slightly in Wales, the major fall (some 6.3 per cent) taking place amongst male full-time employees. This almost certainly reflects the Corus losses alluded to above. Female employment rose in Wales by some 5.7 per cent, with female part-time employment up by 12 per cent. Some commentators

TABLE 12.6
Employment in overseas-owned manufacturing plants in Wales, by unitary
authority, 2000

	Plants	Employees	Percentage of total employees
Blaenau Gwent	24	3198	4.4
Bridgend	18	6660	9.2
Caerphilly	40	6324	8.8
Cardiff	14	3538	4.9
Carmarthenshire	15	3192	4.4
Ceredigion	6	438	0.6
Conwy & Denbighshire	6	1911	2.6
Flintshire	37	5765	8.0
Gwynedd	7	1214	1.7
Isle of Anglesey	6	771	1.1
Merthyr Tydfil	9	1435	2.0
Monmouthshire & Newport	25	7109	9.8
Neath & Port Talbot	15	3582	5.0
Pembrokeshire	5	979	1.4
Powys	9	754	1.0
Rhondda, Cynon, Taff	41	6821	9.4
Swansea	13	2846	3.9
Torfaen	16	4228	5.8
The Vale of Glamorgan	11	4757	6.6
Wrexham	37	6653	9.2
WALES	354	72181	100

Source: Welsh Register of Manufacturing Employment.

have linked the growth in part-time employment to the proliferation of new
call centres across Wales, where the typical employee works flexible part-
time hours.

Once again, as reported before in this review, despite the reported
'strength and tradition' of the manufacturing sector in Wales, this sector saw
a fall of 6.0 per cent to December 2001, equivalent to a further 12,000 jobs.
The fall was greater in percentage terms than that for Great Britain, which
lost 154,000 manufacturing jobs, a fall of some 4.1 per cent. The main
growth sectors in Wales appear to be financial intermediation, which gained
5,000 jobs, and health and social work, which gained 8,000. The service
sector as a whole increased employment to December 2001 by 1.5 per cent,
with the majority of the new positions being taken by women.

Table 12.6 shows the continuing importance of the foreign-owned plants
to the Welsh economy. The figures are the same as those reported last year
and show that in 2000 there were some 354 plants, employing 72,181 people

directly, making up approximately 6 per cent of the employed workforce in Wales. This represents a net fall of 2,069 direct jobs since 1998/9. Of course, many more jobs rely on the presence of these important employers as part of the supply chain that now supports them.

Economic regeneration over the next few years will prioritize activities that lead to job creation and the Single Programming Document (SPD) that supports the case for European Structural Funds stresses this point. Job creation, skills enhancement and the promotion of entrepreneurship are at the heart of many of the Objective 1 projects that have been approved at the time of writing. These include an 'enterprise college' for on-line provision of business start-up skills, a major skills and training grant for North Wales and support for *betterbusineswales.com*, a partnership led by BT and the University of Glamorgan to provide business support and advice for small business owners and budding entrepreneurs. Future projects are also focused on enhancing employability and major infrastructure improvements to allow for new and expanding industries in the more deprived areas of Wales.

UNEMPLOYMENT

Table 12.7 shows regional unemployment rates in the UK over the past ten years. In 1994 Wales had the same rate of unemployment as the UK as a whole. Since then a gap has grown and until 2000 this remained steady at 0.9 percentage points. In 2001 Wales closed this gap to 0.7 percentage points, giving rise to speculation (and indeed some ministerial claims) that the economy was 'improving' at a faster rate than the rest of the UK – thus allowing the politicians to point to the achievable nature of the targets set in their 'Winning Wales' strategy. Unemployment rates have fallen steadily for the UK as a whole and this trend has been reflected in Wales. Examining the change in unemployment rates for other regions, Northern Ireland, Scotland and the North East continue to have higher rates than Wales, although as mentioned all regions witnessed a fall during the year. In the review last year it was noted that the gap between the official rates in Wales and the UK was likely to understate the true differential because the claimant count does not include 'hidden' unemployment, such as various forms of inactivity. This was important because unemployment rates were used by the European Commission to determine the allocation of some structural funds and on this basis some of the parts of the East Wales NUTS 2 region, with low 'official' unemployment rates, were excluded from qualifying for Objective 2 funding.

TABLE 12.7
Annual average unemployment rates, Wales, United Kingdom and regions. Males and females combined, seasonally adjusted, 1992–2001

	1992	1993	1994	1995	1996	1997	1998	1999	2000	2001
South East	8.0	8.6	7.3	5.9	5.0	3.4	2.7	2.4	1.8	1.6
East	8.7	9.4	8.1	6.5	5.9	4.1	3.3	3.0	2.3	2.1
London	10.5	11.6	10.7	9.4	8.5	6.4	5.3	4.8	3.7	3.3
South West	9.2	9.5	8.1	6.8	6.1	4.3	3.5	3.1	2.3	2.1
West Midlands	10.3	10.8	9.9	8.1	7.2	5.5	4.7	4.6	4.1	3.7
East Midlands	9.0	9.5	8.7	7.4	6.7	4.9	4.0	3.8	3.4	3.2
Yorkshire & the Humber	9.9	10.2	9.6	8.5	7.8	6.3	5.5	5.1	4.3	4.0
North West	9.4	9.5	8.7	8.5	7.7	6.0	5.3	4.9	4.2	3.7
North East	12.1	12.9	12.4	11.2	10.2	8.4	7.5	7.2	6.3	5.5
Scotland	9.4	9.7	9.3	7.9	7.6	6.4	5.7	5.4	4.6	4.2
Northern Ireland	13.8	13.7	12.6	11.2	10.7	8.2	7.4	6.5	5.4	5.0
WALES	10.0	10.3	9.3	8.4	8.0	6.4	5.6	5.2	4.5	3.9
UNITED KINGDOM	9.8	10.3	9.3	8.0	7.2	5.5	4.7	4.3	3.6	3.2

Note: Government Office Regions as described for Table 12.1.

Source: *Labour Market Trends.*

TABLE **12.8**
Unemployment: Wales, United Kingdom and regions, Claimants, thousands, not seasonally adjusted, March 2001 and March 2002

| | March 2001 | | | March 2002 | | |
	Male	Female	Total	Male	Female	Total
South East	54.4	17.2	71.6	55.8	18.7	74.4
East	44.9	15.6	60.5	43.7	15.7	59.4
London	116.0	40.4	156.4	120.9	45.7	166.6
South West	43.0	14.9	58.0	41.0	14.1	55.1
West Midlands	81.1	24.6	105.7	74.0	22.8	96.8
East Midlands	52.8	17.5	70.0	47.2	15.8	63.0
Yorkshire & the Humber	81.1	23.3	104.3	73.2	27.7	94.9
North West	104.6	28.6	133.2	99.0	27.5	126.5
North East	54.6	13.7	68.3	50.3	12.8	63.1
Scotland	90.0	25.9	115.8	85.9	24.3	110.2
Northern Ireland	31.1	9.1	40.2	29.2	8.3	37.5
WALES	44.3	13.0	57.2	39.3	11.3	50.6
UNITED KINGDOM	797.5	243.6	1041.1	759.5	238.7	998.2

Note: Government Office Regions as described for Table 12.1.

Source: Labour Market Trends.

Table 12.8 illustrates claimant-count unemployment for the Government Office Regions in the UK in March 2001 and March 2002 (that is, the number of job seekers claiming benefits, broken down by government office region). Every region except London and the South East saw a fall in the number of claimants in the period. In addition, this fall was true in most cases for both males and females, providing further evidence that the economy is continuing to perform well. In Wales the stock of claimants fell by 11.5 per cent, compared to a fall of 4.1 per cent for the UK as a whole. This may be the tentative first sign that Wales has begun to buck the trend of being amongst the lowest-performing regions in the UK. Statistics such as these have been grasped quickly by the Welsh Assembly Government and will certainly require following up as this review develops over the period of structural funding.

Table 12.9 provides information about the age of claimants combined with the duration of spells of unemployment by Government Office Region. The past year has seen a fall in the numbers of 'unemployed for more than one year' category in every Government Office Region. In March 2002 in Wales the percentage of total unemployed who had been out of work for

TABLE **12.9**
Male unemployment by duration and age: Wales, United Kingdom and regions, March 2002

| | Percentage of total unemployed | | |
	Unemployed for over one year	Unemployed for over two years	In 18–24 age group
South East	11.3	4.5	21.8
Eastern	12.4	14.8	23.7
London	19.8	7.4	21.4
South West	11.8	4.3	24.4
West Midlands	18.9	8.4	26.7
East Midlands	15.1	5.9	26.7
Yorkshire & the Humber	15.4	6.0	27.5
North West	16.1	6.3	29.1
North East	17.4	8.0	23.5
Scotland	14.0	5.7	25.9
Northern Ireland	27.6	12.0	28.6
WALES	15.3	6.9	29.8
UNITED KINGDOM	16.3	6.6	25.8

Note: Government Office Regions as described for Table 12.1.

Source: *Labour Market Trends.*

more than one year was 15.3, a fall of 4.8 percentage points over the previous year. In addition, long-term unemployment (those out of work for over two years) also fell in Wales to 6.9 per cent. This adds further weight to the observation last year that the government's New Deal programmes have been successfully reducing the long-term unemployed numbers in the UK.

Table 12.9 shows a far less satisfactory set of statistics for youth unemployment on a UK wide scale. In common with the previous year, 2002 saw an increase in the percentage of unemployed in the 18–24 age group in almost every Government Office Region. In Wales, the figure rose from 26.0 per cent in 2001 to 29.8 in 2002. This evidence of a 3.8 percentage point rise in Wales compared to a 1.4 percentage point rise for the UK as a whole would appear to imply that the Welfare to Work programme has had a lesser effect in Wales than elsewhere in the UK. This is despite the widening of the range of New Deal strands to encompass options such as self-employment, as well as traditional training and business skills.

Table 12.10 reports unemployment rates for Wales by unitary authority. These show the latest figures available at the time of writing, from March 2002, and the unemployment rate is calculated based on estimates of the

TABLE 12.10
Unemployment by Unitary Authority and Wales, unadjusted, workforce base, March 2002

	Male		Female		All	
	Number	Rate	Number	Rate	Number	Rate
Blaenau Gwent	1459	10.7	397	3.6	1856	7.6
Bridgend	1565	5.8	448	1.7	2013	3.8
Caerphilly	2432	7.4	736	2.8	3168	5.3
Cardiff	4456	4.6	1112	1.2	5568	2.9
Carmarthenshire	2080	7.0	630	2.2	2710	4.6
Ceredigion	684	3.7	263	1.7	947	2.8
Conwy	1417	6.6	430	1.9	1847	4.1
Denbighshire	1050	4.6	311	1.5	1361	3.1
Flintshire	1427	3.4	467	1.5	1894	2.6
Gwynedd	2061	7.2	572	2.4	2633	5.0
Isle of Anglesey	1308	9.4	401	3.7	1709	6.9
Merthyr Tydfil	972	8.9	272	2.7	1244	5.9
Monmouthshire	699	3.3	208	1.1	907	2.3
Neath & Port Talbot	1963	6.8	575	2.8	2538	5.1
Newport	2443	5.5	665	1.8	3108	3.8
Pembrokeshire	1821	8.1	553	2.6	2374	5.4
Powys	1034	2.8	405	1.5	1439	2.2
Rhondda, Cynon, Taff	2863	6.4	859	2.2	3722	4.4
Swansea	3350	6.8	859	1.5	4209	4.0
Torfaen	1243	5.8	342	1.7	1585	3.8
The Vale of Glamorgan	1597	5.8	404	1.8	2001	4.0
Wrexham	1364	4.2	396	1.4	1760	2.9
WALES	39288	5.7	11305	1.8	50593	3.9

Source: NOMIS.

Note: Rates are calculated as wholly unemployed claimants as a percentage of the estimated total workforce. All the county rates are calculated using mid-1999-based denominators.

workforce using mid-1999-based denominators. The rates range from 2.2 per cent in Powys to 7.6 per cent in Blaenau Gwent. Every local authority area experienced a fall in the overall rate of unemployment between January 2001 and March 2002 despite job losses indicated in the sections above. In the main cities and towns, Cardiff's rate of unemployment fell from 3.6 per cent to 2.9 per cent, Swansea's fell from 5.3 per cent to 4.0 per cent, Newport's fell from 4.2 per cent to 3.8 per cent and Wrexham's fell from 3.5 to 2.9 per cent. For the rural areas, Ceredigion's fell from 3.6 per cent to 2.8 per cent and Gwynedd's fell back from a high of 6.3 per cent to 5.0 per cent. Male unemployment continues to be a major problem in some areas. Table 12.10

shows that in Blaenau Gwent the rate remains stubbornly above the 10 per cent mark at 10.7. There has been a slight fall in male unemployment in the Isle of Anglesey (9.4 per cent) and Merthyr Tydfil (8.9 per cent) although these remain well above the Welsh average of 5.7 per cent. Female unemployment rates remain much lower, with no UA having a rate above the 3.7 per cent on the Isle of Anglesey (down from 4.9 per cent the previous year).

UA unemployment is the lowest level for which unemployment rates are given because unemployment rates for travel to work areas (TTWAs) are not reported in this section due to the recent debate over the legitimacy of these statistics. The TTWA unemployment rate is defined as the claimant unemployment rate in the area divided by the sum of the employees within the area plus the resident unemployed. Therefore, the unemployment rate in areas with a large number of in-commuters will be underestimated, for example, in urban centres, whereas, the unemployment rate will be overestimated in those areas where there is out-commuting, for example in rural areas. UA unemployment rates are also open to the same argument of self-containment but its effect will be reduced because of the greater geographical size of UAs.

EARNINGS

Pay continues to be one of the major issues that accounts for the relative position of Wales in any comparison of regional performance in the UK. The problem has been described as similar to that of the 'chicken and the egg' – which comes first? The country has, for many years, been seen as one of the main areas for Foreign Direct Investment and has marketed itself externally as having a skilled and adaptable workforce with (relative to other areas of the world) low wages. This has brought inward investors who have established assembly-line plants to produce their goods. However, the types of companies (or divisions of companies) that have not come are those based on higher value-added functions such as research and development. Therefore, the higher-paid workers do not come to Wales or Welsh workers and graduates with these higher level skills migrate out of the country. Therefore, in terms of mainstream assembly and manufacturing jobs, earnings in Wales are at least comparable with the rest of the country. In higher value-added, non-manual sectors the country lags way behind the rest of Great Britain. The figures for earnings are taken from the 2001 *New Earnings Survey* (NES, 2001), an annual survey that provides the most reliable statistical information available on employee wages. The NES does not include earnings of the self-employed and in some cases the sample in smaller unitary authority areas is too small to be reliably reported.

Table 12.11 shows that once again last year Wales lagged behind every other region of Great Britain in terms of earnings, apart from the North East of England. The table gives information on average gross weekly earnings by full-time employees on adult rates in the government office regions for April 2001. The average weekly wage was £381.8 for Welsh employees, an increase of 3.7 per cent over the previous year. This compares with an average of £444.30 in Great Britain, a figure that increased by 8.2 per cent in the year. Much of this large rise was driven by London and the South East. In Wales, employees continue to earn far less than 90 per cent of the average for Great Britain. The gap between Wales and the lowest region (North East) closed to just £1.00. This picture has been relatively constant for the past five years and provides further evidence that the Welsh economy is going to prove extremely difficult to 'move' if the National Assembly economic development targets are going to be met.

The earnings performance of Welsh females has been relatively better than that of the males in recent years and this was again marginally the case in 2001. Last year Welsh male earnings fell well below the North East of England, to become the lowest in Great Britain. Welsh female earnings are relatively better placed although the figures show that Welsh female earnings have slipped from a ranking of seventh to tenth out of the twelve regions. Figures in Table 12.11 suggest that it is in the manual occupations where the traditional strength of earnings for both Welsh male and female employees has been eroded. These levels have now fallen significantly below the national average for the past three years. Manual male earnings are now higher in all eleven other regions than they are in Wales, compared to only eight regions in 2000 and five regions in 1998. Relative earnings in the non-manual occupations remain very low, especially for Welsh males, who again appear at the bottom of the regional earnings table. For females, non-manual earnings were worse in only two other regions, compared to five in 2000 (Scotland having larger increases in earnings than Wales in this area over the year).

Table 12.12 reports the percentage of employees earning less than specified lower earnings thresholds, set at £250 for males and £190 a week for females in 2001. If the story told by Table 12.11 is to be believed then one would expect Welsh employees to be more heavily concentrated at the bottom of the earnings distribution than the other regions. This is

TABLE 12.11
Average gross weekly earnings: Wales, Great Britain and regions, £s, all
industries and services, full-time employees on adult rates, April 2001

	Manual males	Non-manual males	All males	Manual females	Non-manual females	All females	All employees
London	406.9	759.7	667.7	281.9	503.0	483.1	593.7
South East	379.9	607.0	526.6	265.2	401.8	381.6	473.0
East	371.0	561.9	482.9	242.1	378.3	357.5	438.7
South West	343.4	534.8	451.8	235.1	352.1	333.5	408.5
West Midlands	353.2	556.1	462.1	236.4	362.9	340.9	419.1
East Midlands	346.4	506.2	430.9	229.0	346.7	322.3	394.3
Yorkshire & the Humber	345.8	501.5	427.1	222.9	350.8	330.2	392.1
Merseyside	362.7	543.6	462.1	244.8	355.5	342.2	413.8
North West	351.1	533.8	451.1	232.4	355.8	337.2	408.3
North East	356.1	481.3	418.6	225.1	335.3	318.4	380.8
Scotland	349.1	528.9	448.5	233.1	363.9	342.3	404.5
WALES	342.6	478.9	412.3	225.2	346.9	327.4	381.8
GREAT BRITAIN	359.9	582.4	490.5	241.8	388.3	366.8	444.3

Source: *New Earnings Survey*, 2001.

confirmed by the figures which show that Wales had the highest percentage
of male employees in low-paid jobs in 2001, with 19.8 per cent of full-timers
earning less than £250 a week. For manual males, Wales had the highest
concentrations of low-paid workers of any of the regions. In the case of
non-manual males, the North East and Merseyside had a higher percentage
earning less than the threshold. Welsh females fared slightly better as
Yorkshire and the Humber and the North East both had a greater
percentage of their workers earning less than £190 per week. The position of
Welsh non-manual female workers' earnings has fallen back dramatically
this year to become the worst in Great Britain. This is a phenomenon worth
recording and tracking over time because, if the bulk of new employment
generation is (as Table 12.5 suggests) mainly female, the level of pay in these
new jobs appears to be getting far worse. Such a trend can only exacerbate
the degree to which Wales is perceived as a low-pay region and thus
perpetuates the problem of achieving the increases in GDP required by the
EU development programmes.

Table 12.13 examines the average gross weekly earnings in the main
industrial and occupational groupings for Wales and Great Britain. 2001
saw the relative fortunes of both manual and non-manual male Welsh
workers worsen. Manual male production workers in Wales now earn less

TABLE 12.12
Distribution of gross weekly earnings: Wales, Great Britain and regions, £s,
all industries and services, full-time employees on adult rates, April 2001,
percentage with weekly earnings less than £250 for males and less than £190
for females

	Manual males	Non-manual males	All males	Manual females	Non-manual females	All females
London	15.2	5.3	7.9	18.4	3.0	4.4
South East	16.4	8.1	11.0	20.7	5.3	7.6
East	18.2	9.0	12.8	30.1	7.4	10.8
South West	23.0	10.8	16.4	34.4	9.9	13.8
West Midlands	19.9	10.5	14.9	33.2	8.9	13.1
East Midlands	23.2	11.7	17.1	36.1	10.1	15.5
Yorkshire &						
the Humber	23.4	11.9	17.4	38.9	10.1	14.8
Merseyside	23.1	13.5	17.8	24.7	6.0	8.3
North West	22.9	12.0	16.9	34.5	7.9	11.9
North East	22.7	14.9	18.8	42.7	10.1	15.1
Scotland	22.2	10.6	15.8	36.7	7.9	12.6
WALES	27.2	12.7	19.8	36.8	10.4	14.7
GREAT BRITAIN	20.9	9.7	14.3	31.7	7.4	11.1

Source: *New Earnings Survey*, 2001.

than the average for Great Britain, a situation that has occurred only in the
past year. Prior to this, successive reviews have highlighted the fact that
Welsh manufacturing workers earned a little more than the average. This
advantage now appears to have gone. Manual males in production earned
£6.50 less than the national average for such businesses in 2001; this
compares to a situation in 2000 where they earned 30p more. This decline
now appears to be a trend and demonstrates definite erosion of the
competitive advantage that Wales once had in competing for manufacturing
jobs. The *NES 2001* figures suggest that a larger and growing proportion of
production jobs in Wales are low paid and therefore low skill.

In non-manual occupations male workers in Wales continued to perform
badly in comparison with the rest of Great Britain and in 2001 earned on
average only 82.2 per cent of the British figure. Females earned 89.2 per cent
of the comparable national figure, a fall from 93.0 per cent in 2000. Table
12.13 also illustrates significant gaps in relative performance in the service
industries. Non-manual males earn only 80.7 per cent of the GB average, a
significant fall from 86.3 per cent in 2000. The position of females in all

TABLE 12.13

Average gross weekly earnings by broad industry and occupational groupings: Wales and Great Britain, £s, full-time employees on adult rates, April 2001

	Manual males			Non-manual males			Manual females			Non-manual females			All males			All females		
	Wales	GB	% GB	Wales	GB	% GB	Wales	GB	% GB	Wales	GB	% GB	Wales	GB	% GB	Wales	GB	% GB
All industries and services	342.6	359.9	95.2	478.9	582.4	82.2	225.2	241.8	93.1	346.9	388.8	89.2						
All index of production industries	375.9	382.4	98.3	521.5	598.1	87.2	242.7	251.9	96.3	335.0	390.6	85.8						
All manufacturing industries	373.6	378.5	98.7	517.2	592.4	87.3	243.3	251.4	96.8	334.2	390.6	85.6						
All service industries	306.1	337.5	90.7	467.7	579.3	80.7	211.7	236.8	89.4	348.2	389.5	89.4						
All occupations													412.3	490.5	84.1	327.4	366.8	89.3
All manual occupations													342.6	359.9	95.2	225.2	241.8	93.1
All non-manual occupations													478.9	582.4	82.2	346.9	388.8	89.2

Source: New Earnings Survey, 2001.

TABLE 12.14
Average gross weekly earnings, £s, and the 90/10 differential, Wales and Unitary Authorities, all industries and services, full-time employees on adult rates, April 2001

	All employees	90/10 differential
Blaenau Gwent	–	–
Bridgend	379.5	3.14
Caerphilly	372.1	3.13
Cardiff	415.8	3.15
Carmarthenshire	354.0	2.89
Ceredigion	-	-
Conwy	326.0	2.91
Denbighshire	357.0	3.14
Flintshire	420.8	2.97
Gwynedd	353.0	3.25
Isle of Anglesey	–	–
Merthyr Tydfil	–	–
Monmouthshire	–	–
Neath & Port Talbot	417.1	3.21
Newport	388.6	2.99
Pembrokeshire	–	–
Powys	364.2	3.36
Rhondda, Cynon, Taff	356.5	2.96
Swansea	376.6	3.11
Torfaen	375.8	2.70
The Vale of Glamorgan	399.7	3.01
Wrexham	375.6	3.32
WALES	381.8	3.12

Notes: – denotes not available as sample requirements were not met.

Source: *New Earnings Survey*, 2001.

sectors fell slightly over the year and they remain around 11 percentage points lower than the national level.

Table 12.14 illustrates the wide variation of earnings within Wales. Data is presented for all unitary authorities where sample sizes were sufficient in the *NES 2001* to allow for publication. Simple observation of the figures shows the marked difference in average weekly earnings that exists between even neighboring unitary authorities and the skewed distribution of income within authority areas is further highlighted by the 90/10 earnings differential. Earnings data were available for sixteen out of the twenty-two UAs in 2000, with Blaenau Gwent, Ceredigion, Isle of Anglesey, Merthyr Tydfil,

Monmouthshire and Pembrokeshire unable to meet the sampling criteria of the *NES*. Again, in 2001, Neath and Port Talbot had the highest average earnings of the UAs reported, £417 per week, although this again fell short of the GB average of £444. Earnings grew most rapidly in the county of Cardiff. Table 12.14 also shows that Swansea remains below the Welsh average with earnings of £376.6. Conwy remained the UA with lowest average earnings of all at £326.0 a week.

The 90/10 earnings differential, which is expressed as the earnings figure exceeded by the top 10 per cent of workers divided by the respective figure for the bottom 10 per cent, increased slightly in 2001 to 3.12 from 3.10 in 2000. This simple measure suggests that earnings inequality increased very slightly in 2001. Looking at the county based data, earning inequality worsened in Blaenau Gwent, Flintshire, Newport, Rhondda Cynon Taff, Swansea, Torfaen and Wrexham. In the remaining authority areas the inequality was reduced slightly.

A major drawback of the *NES* data published in the tables is that they exclude part-time workers altogether and miss out many of those with low wages because they only cover full-time workers who earn in excess of the lower earnings limit. The tables (and the survey itself) also ignore the self-employed on the grounds that earnings data from this group is highly unreliable. Unfortunately, the problem of 'missing data' is important for Wales, where the proportion of part-time employees is higher and wages are lower than the national averages. The true position in Wales is therefore likely to be worse than that shown.

HOUSE PRICES

The past year has seen another extraordinary rise in house prices across the UK. As Table 12.15 illustrates from the Halifax Bank House Price Index, the average rise has been 5.7 per cent to the end of the first quarter of 2002, but these changes are very different across the regions.

Prior to the relatively rapid rise in house prices over the past two years there have been three distinct periods of high house-price inflation since 1970. The first, in the early 1970s, coincided with the oil crisis and a period of exceptionally high retail price inflation. The second period occurred at the end of the 1970s and the third at the end of the 1980s. The mid- and late 1980s housing boom culminated in annual house-price inflation reaching a peak of 34 per cent in October 1988, marking a doubling in house prices in just four and a half years. Prices in Wales increased by 104 per cent between

TABLE 12.15
Average house prices, first quarter 2002, United Kingdom, regions and former Welsh counties

Regions of the UK	£	Annual % change	Welsh counties and cities[a]	£
South East	153992	13.1	South Glamorgan	107300
East Anglia	109166	20.8	Gwent	74900
South West	112924	21.9	Clwyd	66250
West Midlands	94664	17.3	Mid Glamorgan	60800
East Midlands	84509	19.2	West Glamorgan	58000
Yorkshire & Humberside	64941	16.5	Dyfed	53750
North West	71663	16.1	Gwynedd	65200
North	64436	13.8	Cardiff	112800
Scotland	61061	8.3	Newport	83200
Northern Ireland	71749	-2.7	Swansea	63750
WALES	63619	12.9	Wrexham	67400
UNITED KINGDOM[b]	86196	16.2		

Notes: a – Counties' figures are average semi-detached prices.
 b – Excludes Northern Ireland.

Source: Halifax House Price Index.

mid-1985 and early 1990. The subsequent fall in prices began in mid-1989, and prices remained on a downward trend for the next six years before reaching a trough in July 1995. Average UK prices fell by 12 per cent overall during this period. Prices in Wales fell by 14 per cent between the first quarter of 1990 and the second quarter of 1995. This has been the only period since 1970 when house prices have fallen in 'nominal' (or monetary) as well as 'real' (that is, once adjusted for retail price inflation) terms.

House prices returned to their late 1980s peak in January 1998 and have subsequently risen by a further 41 per cent. Annual house-price inflation reached 16 per cent in January 2000 before easing during the remainder of 2000. Falling interest rates stimulated a renewed pick-up with inflation returning to double digits in the second half of 2001. House prices in Wales have risen by 28 per cent over the past three years, ranking the country seventh out of the twelve UK regions.

The current house price boom is a very interesting phenomenon to study. Demand in the larger conurbations is clearly outstripping supply and buyers appear to need to move quickly to secure a property. This is tending to inflate prices and first-time buyers are finding it increasingly difficult to purchase property within the city locations. In order to enter the market, buyers increasingly have to move further out into the commuter belts.

Prices and demand for property continue to rise in and around major cities, towns and the M4 corridor. There is evidence to show that South Wales is benefiting from a 'ripple-effect' caused by burgeoning prices in the South West, particularly Bristol and Bath. Cardiff remains a high-price area, with the average house price now in excess of £110,000. In the Swansea area, the market has slowed down, with an increasing number of buyers making initial enquiries, but estate agents report that sales are not following through in similar numbers. Valley communities have seen little change in property values with many of the areas bracing themselves for job losses. To the north, the popularity of Flintshire for commuters from Liverpool and the North West continues to be reflected in higher prices.

The figures for county variations in Table 12.15 continue to show evidence of a North–South and East–West divide in Wales. The Halifax Bank figures show that along the M4 corridor in south Wales, average prices for a semi-detached property are £112,800 in Cardiff and £83,200 in Newport. In Wrexham in the north, the same property would cost £67,400.

COMPETITIVENESS

This section considers the most recent data from the Department of Trade and Industry's (DTI) Regional Competitiveness Indicators (September 2001). In this year's review there are data series from 1997 through to May 2001 which summarize the variables considered by the DTI to be most important in making regional comparisons of this sort. These are gross domestic product (GDP) per head, household disposable income per head, gross value added per head, total income support claimants and manufacturing investment by foreign and UK-owned companies.

GDP and Household Disposable Income measure different aspects of a region's income. The former gives an indication of the size of the local economy – regardless of where the income from that economy accrues – and the latter gives an indication of the income residents within regions have to spend on goods and services.

GDP per head is here repeated in index form from Table 12.1. It is measured as the income of those working in a region including commuters (workplace basis) and these data are used in international comparisons at sub-national level because they are readily available internationally. Wales has the third lowest GDP per head figure (some 80.5 per cent of the UK average), after Northern Ireland and the North East, of all regions in the UK in 1999. The 'Winning Wales' targets are for this gap to narrow to only 10 percentage points. Such a change means that Wales must grow on average by approximately 1 per cent per annum more rapidly than the average for the rest of the UK. Such a growth rate, which to date has not been achieved by Wales, is one that this review must track carefully over the coming years.

Household Disposable Income is here again defined according to ESA95. The figures are for 1999 and show that Wales has a level of 90.4 per cent of the UK average, above that for Northern Ireland and the North East. As the above section on earnings discussed, income levels in Wales continue to lag behind other UK regions and the reduction of unemployment over the last year appears to have been achieved without a consequent increase in relative earnings.

Gross Value Added per employee is the official competitiveness measure of labour productivity in manufacturing for each region. The figures are for 1999 and show Wales with a level of 80.5 per cent of the UK average. In a similar way to Household Income, Wales ranks below all other regions except for Northern Ireland and the North East. This clearly indicates that value added remains a major problem when targets for economic regeneration are set.

The number of Income Support Claimants is a measure of social deprivation in a region. The indicator used shows the number of Income Support Claimants as a proportion of the population aged over sixteen. Since the introduction of the Job Seekers Allowance the figures for the unemployed are no longer included in the Income Support Claimant figures. This has resulted in the figures being between 3 and 6 percentage points lower than those published earlier in the series. In May 2001, Wales had 10.1 per cent of the population claiming income support, compared with the UK average of 8.4 per cent. This figure was slightly up from one year ago, suggesting a slight worsening in this measure which ties in with the discussion of unemployment measures above.

Manufacturing Investment and Output by Foreign-owned Companies is a measure of the attractiveness of a region to foreign investors and the importance of foreign investment to the manufacturing base of a region. Table 12.16 shows the same figures as were presented in last year's review. In 1997 nearly £13.6 billion was invested in the UK, almost half of which was from foreign-owned companies. Investment is measured by Net Capital Expenditure. Individual yearly data should be treated with caution as large one-off investment decisions by companies can make significant differences

TABLE 12.16
Regional Competitiveness Indicators

Region	GDP per head (UK=100) 1999	Household Disposable Income per head (UK=100) 1999	Gross Value Added per head (UK=100) 1999	Total Income Support Claimants (proportion of population over 16) % May 2001	Manufacturing Investment by Foreign and UK-owned Companies (£million) 1997	
					Foreign	UK
London	130.0	119.4	146.3	9.9	450	849
South East	116.4	111.6	110.2	5.6	862	1286
East	116.2	111.7	103.6	6.4	566	1035
South West	90.8	97.5	90.8	6.7	451	977
West Midlands	91.7	91.2	91.7	8.9	1000	1482
East Midlands	93.6	92.7	93.6	7.5	500	1162
Yorkshire & the Humber	87.9	92.3	87.9	9.0	245	1487
North West & Merseyside	86.9	93.0	86.9	10.6	701	2050
North East	77.3	82.9	77.3	11.0	369	774
England	102.4	101.6	102.4	8.3	5145	11102
Scotland	96.5	94.8	96.5	10.1	682	1212
Northern Ireland	77.5	85.9	77.5	13.7	112	378
WALES	80.5	90.4	80.5	10.1	539	888
UNITED KINGDOM	100	100	100	8.4	6478	13579

Source: Regional Competitiveness Indicators, DTI, Sept 2001.

to total investment figures in a particular region. This indicator only covers manufacturing; a comparison with the service sector is not possible due to lack of data.

OVERVIEW

The economic commentary this year paints a picture of a Wales that is changing quite markedly over time. The statistics throw up snapshots of parts of the economy that appear to be operating in quite different ways. Employment is rising, unemployment is falling, yet relative wages continue to worsen. In the midst of a housing boom, consumer spending remains high, interest rates remain at a historic low, but inflation at the time of writing has fallen to less than 1.5 per cent.

A great deal of the emphasis of economic development, at least in public and in the press, has been focused on enterprise and entrepreneurship. The 'Winning Wales' strategy has now committed to the full funding of the Entrepreneurship Action Plan (EAP) for Wales. This has been joined by the Knowledge Exploitation Fund (KEF), a £28m ELWa project that aims to embed enterprise education into the further and higher education sectors. Indeed, all further education and higher education institutions now have their own 'Entrepreneurship Champion', whose role is to do just that. Finance Wales plc has been established as a subsidiary of the WDA to provide risk capital for new and expanding ventures and to plug the funding gap identified by the EAP. The fundamental challenge remains for all of these bodies to make the European Structural Funds work and to put in place a system of monitoring and regulation that will allow the approved projects to achieve their aims. Wales is now almost three years into the new funding arrangements and the first period of evaluation is with us. It will be interesting to chart the progress of these high profile initiatives as data becomes available from this exercise over the next year.

REFERENCES

National Assembly for Wales (NAW) (2001). *A Winning Wales: The National Economic Development Strategy of the Welsh Assembly Government*, Cardiff, NAW.
http://www.wales.gov.uk/themesbudgetandstrategic/content/neds/index.html
National Assembly for Wales (NAW) (2000). *Entrepreneurship Action Plan*, Cardiff, NAW.
Department of Trade and Industry (DTI) (2001). *Regional Competitiveness Indicators*, September.

Contemporary Wales is now *freely* available online to all subscribers

CatchWord

Benefits include:

- Document to document linking via references for fast reliable access to the wider literature
- Fully searchable across full text, abstracts, text, titles, TOC and figures delivering comprehensive search results
- Links to and from major Abstract and Indexing resources to aid research
- Full text searching across multiple journals for a wider view of the research that counts
- TOC alerting service keeping you up to date with the latest research

Set up Access now at:

- www.catchword.com and follow the online instructions

Not a subscriber? Why not find out more by contacting press@press.wales.ac.uk

CatchWord Enquiries:
support@catchword.com

A TOLERANT NATION?
exploring ethnic diversity in Wales

Edited by
Charlotte Williams, Neil Evans and Paul O'Leary

approx pp 244   216x138mm   February 2003
paperback   **£14.99**   ISBN 0-7083-1759-6

Wales is a changing nation. It incorporates peoples of different inheritances, backgrounds and perspectives, all of whom will contribute to shaping the nation's future. *A Tolerant Nation?* presents the first overview of the past two hundred years of ethnic diversity in Wales and demonstrates the significance of this diversity for understanding contemporary Wales.

In addition to providing a historical context for understanding Welsh multiculturalism, the essays collected here also discuss dominant views of ethnic diversity in Wales and the ways in which the Welsh themselves have been conceived of as an ethnic minority, both within and outside Wales. Individual essays reflect on issues such as the literary representation of race, Welsh missionary activities, racial tensions, refugees and asylum seekers in Wales, and the question of equality.

A Tolerant Nation? illustrates the significant contribution of ethnic minorities in Wales to the development of Welsh economic, social and cultural life. It offers a revealing insight into the rich diversity of contemporary Wales, and fills a glaring gap in current research on the state of the devolved nation.

Charlotte Williams is a Lecturer in Social Policy at the University of Wales, Bangor.
Neil Evans is Honorary Research Fellow in the School of History and Archaeology, Cardiff University, as well as joint editor of *Llafur: The Journal of Welsh People's History*.
Paul O'Leary lectures in the Department of History and Welsh History at the University of Wales, Aberystwyth.

University of Wales Press
FREEPOST (CF. 1529), Cardiff CF10 4ZX
Tel: 029 2049 6899 (24 hours)   *Fax:* 029 2049 6108
www.wales.ac.uk/press

Scottish Affairs is the definitive forum for comment and debate on Scottish politics, society and current affairs. It is published in book form every quarter and is independent of political parties and pressure groups. Each year, one of the issues focuses on a particular theme. These have included:

Scotland, Quebec and Catalonia
Gender and National Identity
Understanding Constitutional Change (a complete special issue)
The Northern Ireland Agreement
Social Inclusion

Annual Subscription (four issues):
£27.50 (individuals), £45.00 (institutions)

Published by and further information (including how to join our electronic mailing list) from:

Unit for the Study of Government in Scotland
University of Edinburgh
Chisholm House
High School Yards
Edinburgh
EH1 1LZ

Tel: 0131 650 2456
Fax: 0131 650 6345
Email: Ladams@ed.ac.uk